Tales
out
of
School

Compiled by
Pat Edwards & Wendy Body

Acknowledgements

We are grateful to the following for permission to reproduce copyright material: The Bodley Head on behalf of the author/Viking Penguin, Inc for an extract from the story *The Cartoonist* by Besty Byars; the author, Bill Boyle for his poems 'Dead Good' and 'Beg, borrow or ...'; William Collins Sons & Co Ltd for extracts from *The Whizzkids Handbook 2* by Peter Eldin and an extract from *Anastasia Krupnik* by Lois Lowry; the author, Peter Combe for the words and music of his song 'When I'm Thirteen' from *The ABC Sing Together 82;* C J Fulcher on behalf of the authors for the poems 'Days' by Lucy Bassett and 'Outside at Lunchtime' by Tina Clarke from *First Year Poetry Anthology 1986-87* compiled by C J Fulcher, produced by Chepstow Comprehensive School; the author's agents on behalf of Haytul Pty Ltd for the poem 'Revenge' by Robin Klein; Oxford University Press Australia for an extract from *Adventures With My Worst Best Friend* by Max Dann, copyright Max Dann 1982; Penguin Books Ltd for the story 'Send Three and Fourpence We are Going to a Dance' from *Nothing to be Afraid Of* by Jan Mark (Kestrel Books 1980), copyright © Jan Mark, 1977, 1980 and for the poem 'Picking Teams' from *Please Mrs Butler* by Allan Ahlberg (Kestrel Books, 1983), © 1983 by Allan Ahlberg; Penguin Books Australia Ltd for an extract from *Hating Alison Ashley* by Robin Klein.

We are grateful to the following for permission to reproduce photographs: Adams Picture Library, pages 25 *below left,* 26 *centre right,* 26 *below right;* John Birdsall, pages 24/25 *background,* 24 *above right,* 25 *above right,* 26/27 *background,* 26 *above left* and *right,* 26 *below left;* Sally and Richard Greenhill, pages 24 *left,* 24 *below right,* 25 *above left,* 25 *below right,* 27; Jan Mark, page 46 (photo Peter Greenland). Cover photographs: John Birdsall.

Illustrators, other than those acknowledged with each story, include Donna Gynall p.23; Pauline Turney pp.28-9; Azoo pp.30-1 and 103-5; Louise Metcalf pp.32-3; Sylvia Witte pp.34-5; Peter Edwards pp.46-7; Rebecca Pannell pp.48-9; Rachel Legge pp.78-9; Melissa Webb pp.80-1; Lorraine Ellis pp.82-3; Rolf Heimann pp.84-7; Sara Woodward pp.110-12.

Contents

Showing up Alison Ashley! *Robin Klein*   4

Revenge! *Robin Klein*   23

School days   24

Days *Lucy Bassett*   28

Outside at Lunchtime *Tina Clarke*   29

Hey! Heard this one?   30

Dead good *Bill Boyle*   32

Beg, borrow or . . . *Bill Boyle*   33

Special days: May Day   34

Send Three and Fourpence We are Going to a Dance
   Jan Mark   36

Meet an author: Jan Mark   46

Excuses for being late *Peter Eldin*   48

The ideal school timetable   49

F for . . . Fail? *Lois Lowry*   50

Bottom of the class   65

No Art in Maths! *Betsy Byars*   66

Alfie's cartoons   75

Meet a cartoonist: Peter Foster   76

What shall I be?   78

A recipe for paper   80

How the secret spread   81

Make your own paper   82

Who invented pens . . . and pencils?   84

Leaving Home *Max Dann*   88

When I'm Thirteen *Peter Combe*   102

How to stay unhealthy!   104

Worst Friend or Best Enemy? *Aesop*   106

Picking Teams *Allan Ahlberg*   110

Words to pick *Glossary*   111

SHOWING UP ALISON ASHLEY!

Erica Yurken (nickname "Yuk") never had any doubts about her own genius. She considered herself the only genius at Barringa East Primary (even if her teachers didn't always notice!). It had been easy for Erica to feel superior to other kids like poor dim Margaret Collins (who still spells her name Margeart even though she's in Grade 6) and arch-enemy Barry Hollis (who never does any work and steals any school property not nailed down!).

Erica did everything better than anyone else in her class at Barringa East ... that is, until Alison Ashley came. Alison excelled at everything. She was beautiful, rich, clever and as well-behaved as a nativity angel. But Erica was determined to show up Alison Ashley ...

PART I

"I'll show Alison Ashley, the new girl, how to work the camera," I said. I really enjoyed showing people new things. It was a very satisfying feeling if they didn't catch on to instructions right away, and you could say, "There's not much point in showing you. I'm sorry, but certain things are just beyond the scope of some people."

But Alison put up her hand. She always put up her hand before she talked in class, and in Barringa East Primary it looked peculiar, this solitary, straight-as-a-flagpole hand up in the air, when everyone else was just calling out. Miss Lattimore nodded approvingly at her, and Alison said she already knew how to work an Olympus Trip camera, also a movie camera, and she'd already had some dark-room lessons at her last school. She didn't sound as though she was actually showing off. She was pleasant and polite as always, but I felt extremely irritated. Up to then I'd been the only student at Barringa East who knew that the red light over the dark-room door wasn't there just to teach the prep kids traffic drill.

"Well then, having someone with experience will make our photography programme more interesting," said Miss Lattimore. "Especially for the members of this class who already think they know it all and can't be taught any more by anyone." (Naturally she meant Barry Hollis, although she was looking in my direction. Perhaps the look was meant to include approval of me as well as Alison Ashley, as I helped supervise the school photography programme. I often turned up early and changed the corridor displays without waiting to be asked, to save Miss Lattimore the bother of doing it herself.)

Out in the playground, Barry Hollis suggested photographing the girls coming out of the boys' toilets and the boys coming out of the girls' toilets, but Miss Lattimore just looked at him witheringly. Margeart Collins had the first dithery turn with the camera. She tried to take a picture of a sparrow, but it flew off before she even worked out where the viewfinder was. "Never mind, Margaret," said Miss Lattimore. "Maybe it will turn out to be a very nice picture of Twisty crumbs on asphalt."

Kevin Cossan took a corny shot of Lisa making out she was shooting a netball goal. The next six people had similar tired ideas. No one else in our grade except me had any imagination whatever. Then it was Alison's turn with the camera.

She had her picture all worked out. She squinted through the viewfinder judging angles, only of course Alison Ashley didn't really squint, she just peeped prettily. She climbed up the ladder of the suspended tunnel bridge made of old car tyres, and took a slow, careful photograph. Everyone jeered about how dumb it was, photographing a lot of old tyres. But I looked over her shoulder and saw that the tyres curved into a wonderful pattern of light and shade. I wished jealously that I had thought of it first.

"That's very good, Alison," Miss Lattimore said. "It's nice to find someone who can keep her eyes open and find something out of the ordinary." Alison wound on the film and handed me the camera.

I went twice round the oval peeping prettily at various things through the viewfinder, and came back. "About time, too!" kids snarled impatiently. "Come on, Yuk, hand it over."

"I haven't taken my picture yet," I said.

"Honestly," said Miss Lattimore. "You are . . ."

"But I've thought of something very artistic," I said. "I'm going to take a close-up picture of bark."

The immature people in our grade sat up and dangled their paws and yapped. "Stop that silly yelping," Miss Lattimore said angrily. "And Barry Hollis, you stupid boy, untie Margaret from that goal post at once. I've told you before not to take macrame string from the craft room."

I went hunting for a tree with suitable artistic bark. It took a long time. There weren't many trees in our playground on account of the Eastside Boys ripping up shrubs as quickly as the parents' club put them in. But there was one eucalyptus tree near the fence.

I enjoyed taking photographs; a camera always made
me feel like a newspaper reporter, as though I had done
a lot of slick dangerous living and worked in a skyscraper.
I took pictures of the tree from every possible angle, and
somehow used up all the film in the camera.

I didn't really mean to, but Miss Lattimore turned
very snitchy when she saw that the dial was at thirty-six.
Everyone carried on about missing out, although it
would have been a waste of good film, anyhow, letting
them have a try. Their idea of taking pictures was to
snap each other pulling down the red part of their
eyelids.

"Next art session the people with worthwhile negatives can prepare a really good print for the competition," Miss Lattimore said when she was through telling me off. "Barry Hollis, get off that rubbish-bin lid at once and let that person out. Don't be so unhygienic."

We went back to our room for lunch and Alison got out her smart white lunchbox. This time she had a wholemeal salad roll practically hopping out of its compartment with vitamins, an apple polished like a Christmas-tree ornament, a health bar made out of sesame seeds, wheatgerm and honey, and a drink bottle filled with tomato juice.

My lunch was weird, as it usually was on the days I brought it from home instead of buying it. I hadn't been able to find any lunchwraps, so I'd put it all into a used waxed cornflakes bag. I had a thawed-out, pre-cooked frozen rissole, an Irish stew sandwich, and a grotty looking pear, which looked dead on the outside, but was okay in the middle. Some cornflakes were stuck to its skin. I saw Alison Ashley look at it in disbelief and flinch.

Miss Belmont was putting notices up in the corridor, so it was possible to talk. "Are you going to the high school or the tech next year, Alison?" I asked out of curiosity. Our local high school had even a worse name than Barringa East Primary. Everyone said they flushed the heads of new kids in the toilets as a welcoming ceremony on their first day. The tech was where my sister Valjoy went. They'd turned it into a co-ed school two years ago, and still had only a small enrolment of girls, which was why Valjoy chose it instead of the high school. Parents were a bit nervous about sending their girls to the tech, as it had even a worse name than Barringa East Primary and the high school put together. But Valjoy enjoyed being the only female in the metal-welding class. She liked being outnumbered by a vast horde of wild and daring boys.

"I won't be going to either," Alison said. "My mother put my name down for Kyle Grammar School. She tried to get them to take me earlier, when we found out about the new school zoning. But they didn't have a vacancy till next year."

A bit of cold Irish stew sandwich stuck in my throat. You could see Kyle Girls Grammar School from the train going into town. It was just like a school out of an English story book. The girls there wore beautiful pale-blue uniforms with little navy-blue bowler hats and gloves, and if they travelled on the train they always stood up for adults. Once when I was in the same carriage with a couple of them, they found this paper bag with a bottle of expensive skin-moisturising lotion on the seat, and they handed it in to the station attendant. I was so impressed by such honesty that I told Valjoy when I got home. But she went straight up to the station and asked if anyone had handed in a bottle of skin moisturizer because she'd bought some for her Gran's birthday and left it in a carriage, and they gave it to her.

Every time I looked out of the train and saw Kyle Grammar School I ached with jealousy. I would have adored to go to a school like that, and wear a Latin motto on my blazer pocket. And end up as a prefect, or better still, the head girl. At Barringa High School they'd given up trying to make the kids wear uniforms years ago, and I didn't think they'd ever had prefects, because the kids there didn't take notice of the teachers, let alone other kids. I was sure I'd fit into a school like Kyle without any difficulty at all. It wasn't fair that I'd never be able to go there. Alison Ashley already had everything, and Kyle Girls Grammar School, too, to look forward to next year.

"Oh, that place," I said airily. "They don't teach you anything there except how to cook for dinner parties and play tennis. I'll be going to Barringa High. From choice. They've got a new science block, and a choice of five languages, and for sport they do scuba diving, and they have sit-in strikes and mass demonstrations and lots of other interesting things."

So there, Alison Ashley, I thought. Swallow that along with your old vitamins.

"You're wrong about Kyle," Alison said. "It had the highest HSC results of any school in the state last year."

So there, Erica Yurken, her blue eyes said. Eat that along with your disgusting old pear, you mouldy peasant.

"Barringa High School has a computer room," I said. "And it also has a drama course. They give a big concert every year, and last year they did *Arsenic and Old Lace*." I didn't tell her that the performance was cancelled because the Eastside Boys broke into the assembly hall beforehand and did something peculiar to the lighting.

"Well, at Kyle you can study ballet," she said. "Oh, I meant to tell you. You made the shoes look funny, on those ballet girls you drew for your assignment. They don't have a whole lot of criss-crosses. Balletshoe ribbons just cross over once and wrap around the ankle."

"Not always," I said, "I went to a ballet last year, a proper one, not just *Peter and the Wolf*. It was a famous Russian ballet company doing *Swan Lake*, and they had their ribbons crossing over and over right up to their knees. Pale blue ribbons to match their dresses."

Alison didn't say anything in her usual annoying way, but she raised her eyebrows.

"I went backstage after the performance," I said. "I know a lot of people in the theatre. And I was allowed to help those ballerinas take off their ballet slippers and pack them away ready to go back to Russia."

"It must have been a very peculiar *Swan Lake*," said Alison. "They always wear white in *Swan Lake*. As far as I know swans aren't ever blue. And they certainly wouldn't have had their ballet slipper ribbons going right up to their knees."

I bit savagely into my pear, which collapsed messily. I didn't have anything to clean it off the desk with except my half-eaten Irish stew sandwich. "You just think you're great, Alison Ashley!" I said, exploding like my pear. "You think you know everything! You think you're great just because you live over on Hedge End Road!"

"I've got to live somewhere, haven't I?" she said snappily. "And do you mind wiping your lunch off my folder cover, if it's not too much trouble?"

Dianne and Leanne and Bev and everyone looked at us with interest. You can't mistake a fight shaping up promisingly in a class room.

"You think you're so fantastic!" I said. "You look down your nose at everyone and everything in this school! You snob!"

"Good on yer, Yuk," said Barry Hollis.

"You mind your own business, Barry Hollis, and stay out of private conversations," I said coldly.

"I am not a snob!" Alison said. "What about you, anyhow, showing off all the time! You've done nothing except show off ever since I came to this school!"

"Yeah," said Barry Hollis. "Good on yer, Alison Ashley!"

"You mind your own business and keep out of private conversations," Alison said, and her voice wasn't polite and quiet anymore, it was all over the place and high up, like mine.

Miss Belmont came in and stared at us. Alison busily fitted the lids on her lunchbox and drink bottle. I dumped my pear-flavoured Irish stew Wettex into the waxed cornflake bag, and twisted it up viciously.

"Grade six, you may go out to play, now," Miss Belmont said.

I went along to the sick bay instead and asked Mrs Orlando if I could have some of the new brand of ear drops and an antacid tablet. She told me to put a bit of cottonwool in my ear if it was hurting, and not to gobble my lunch and I wouldn't get indigestion. "Go outside and play in the fresh air, Yuk," she said, not even looking up from her Gestetner machine.

Mrs Orlando was a lousy sick-bay attendant.

Alison and I didn't speak to each other for a whole week.

Every day she wore something new to school and every day her work folder collected A's and flattering comments from Miss Belmont. All the teachers doted on her in a very sickening manner. At assembly they'd be hectoring their classes into what passed for straight lines at Barringa East Primary, and they'd turn and look at Alison Ashley standing there as polite and nicely brought up as a nativity angel, and their eyes would glimmer with faint hope for the human race. Maybe they thought Alison's excellent qualities would spread around the whole school and infect everyone, like gastroenteritis.

But it was peculiar, because none of the other kids took to her at all. She was just so private and never started conversations or yakked on about herself. So everyone sort of skated warily around her, not stirring her, because kids who were that pretty and that well dressed didn't get stirred. But they acted as though she didn't really belong to our school at all, as though she was just a visitor.

The same way they treated me.

PART II

"I've developed the film with the competition photographs on it," said Miss Lattimore in our next lesson. "You'll have to get cracking, grade six, to print your entry pictures in time. This is your last art lesson before the school camp."

Our grade certainly contained a lot of dense people.

"What competition?" asked Wendy Millson.

"What film?" asked Col.

"What photos?" asked Lisa.

"What's developing and printing?" asked Margeart Collins.

"You know very well what I mean," said Miss Lattimore, and her voice took on a high-pitched brittle sound. "The photographs we took in the playground last week for the interschool competition."

"Oh, those," said everyone, and went on throwing pellets of clay at each other.

"The people who want to enter for the competition may go into the dark-room and make a print from their negative," said Miss Lattimore. "And after it's washed and dried, mount it nicely on some cardboard, and make sure none of the glue seeps around the edges, and print your name, age, grade and school on the back, and . . . "

Most of the kids stopped listening at the first hint that the competition meant work. Barry Hollis hadn't started to listen in the first place. He was doing what he always did in art/craft, and that was see how much school property he could pinch without being caught. His cheeks were bulging with cutout copper enamelling shapes, ready to spit out into his hankie when Miss Lattimore was looking the other way. He sold them to kids after school for five cents each.

"Barry Hollis, what's the meaning of that insolent face?" Miss Lattimore demanded angrily. "I'm just about fed up with you wasting time in this class. Mr Nicholson said to send you over to the office if I had any more trouble with you this week. Well, what have you got to say for yourself, young man?"

Barry Hollis couldn't say anything without copper horse-shoes and little copper butterflies skittering out of his mouth if he opened it. So he just stared at Miss Lattimore right between her two eyes with this sinister look he could put on that always terrified new teachers. But Miss Lattimore had been teaching at Barringa East Primary for nearly two years, and her tolerance level for Barry Hollis had slowly increased over that period. I guess teachers just had to increase their tolerance levels with Barry Hollis, or they would have ended up in prison for murder.

"All right," said Miss Lattimore. "If you refuse to answer when I speak to you, you can just go over and tell Mr Nicholson you've been insolent again. No doubt he'll bear that in mind when he's finalising the list for the grade six camp. Erica, you go with him to make sure he gets there."

Someone always had to accompany Barry Hollis to the office, otherwise he just climbed over the fence and went home. Or he went down behind the sports shed and had a smoke, or caught the bus over to the shopping centre for a spot of shoplifting.

Barry Hollis tilted his sinister expression in my direction. I put up my hand—I was copying that from Alison Ashley—and told Miss Lattimore that I preferred not to escort him to the office all by myself. Last time I did, he tried to hang me up on one of the corridor pegs by the hood of my tracksuit.

"Very well. Alison, you go, too," said Miss Lattimore. She gave Barry Hollis one last cold dismissing look, but while she was speaking to Alison, he'd managed to grab a stack of coloured paper and some sheets of Letraset and slide them under his shirt.

Outside in the corridor he spat out the copper shapes and put them in his pocket, where he already had some brand new tubes of epoxy resin. Then he pulled out a packet of cigarettes. "Want a smoke?" he asked Alison, showing off.

"I'm not allowed to smoke," she said simply.

Now most kids would never come out with a statement like that. They'd rather say, "Oh, I gave up smoking last week". Or, "I don't smoke that brand". Or, "I've got a sore throat". That was the first time I ever heard any kid at our school come right out and say they weren't allowed.

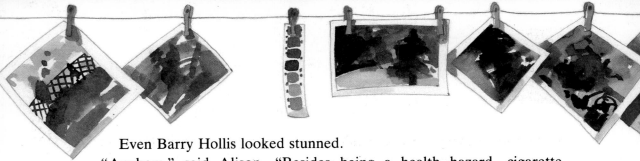

Even Barry Hollis looked stunned.

"Anyhow," said Alison. "Besides being a health hazard, cigarette smoke smells awful. I don't like being close to people who smoke."

Barry Hollis did a peculiar thing. He put the unlit cigarette back in his pocket. It was just as well he did, because Miss Belmont came out of the staff room and wanted to know why he was being sent to the office under escort. Barry Hollis said what he always said to teachers who asked questions like that, which was, "That's for me to know and you to find out".

I took one look at Miss Belmont's expression and grabbed Alison by the arm and whisked her back into the art and craft room. Only fools would choose to hang around when volcanoes are about to erupt.

Then I became aware that I was actually touching Alison Ashley, the Snow Queen, and you don't touch people who are your enemy. So I quickly took my hand away and wiped it on my skirt.

Miss Lattimore already had the dark-room set up. "Alison and Yuk, you two can get started on your prints," she said.

I picked up the strip of negatives and placed it in the enlarger. Shane Corbert had produced his usual blurry failure. Margeart, as well as scaring away the sparrow, had also managed to get a blobby image of her thumb. Someone else, Barry Hollis probably, had taken a picture of a bottom bending over in tight jeans. I moved the strip of negatives along and came to the one Alison had taken of the tyres.

"You can go first and get your funny little picture done," I said. "I like to spend a lot of time without any distractions when I work. Now, this machine is called an enlarger, and this knob here is the focuser, and this little switch is what you use to turn the red shutter on and off . . ."

"I know all that already," said Alison Ashley. "You're not the only person in the world who knows about photography."

She fiddled around making test strips on different grades of paper. Then she made one large print, developed it and put it in the tray of fixer, doing

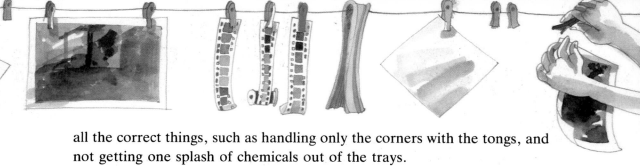

all the correct things, such as handling only the corners with the tongs, and not getting one splash of chemicals out of the trays.

"It's been in long enough to have a look at it under white light," she said.

White light, indeed! Nobody else except Miss Lattimore called it that. I switched on the overhead light and looked over her shoulder stealthily, because I certainly didn't want to give her the impression of being interested in anything that she did.

The picture was marvellous.

Everything was perfect, the shadows crisp and dark, every little detail sharp. It didn't look a bit like a snapshot of old playground equipment. It looked just like a picture you would pay a lot for if it was poster sized in a newsagency.

Miss Lattimore came in and raved about it, practically with tears of pride running down her suntan. "It's really wonderful, Alison," she cried ecstatically. (I'd noticed before that art/craft teachers at our school always carried on like that if anyone ever produced something that looked even vaguely artistic.) "It's really excellent work for someone your age," Miss Lattimore burbled. "When it's been washed and dried, you must take it over and show Mr Nicholson."

In fact, all the teachers at Barringa East Primary carried on like that. Every time any kid produced something that was tidy, clean, completed or even recognisable as work, they'd be sent over to show it to Mr Nicholson. Maybe the teachers felt sorry for him, having to go along to seminars with all the other principals from schools like Gilland, Edgeworth and Jacana Heights.

I felt jealous. All through my years at Barringa East Primary, from prep grade up, I'd always been the one sent to show work to Mr Nicholson. "Right," I thought, when they both went out to wash Alison's marvellous print. "This is where I show Alison Ashley what real photography is all about."

I found my negatives of bark, and projected the first one to the largest possible size. If I'd known how to project it right down on to the floor to make it poster size, even if I had to use the photo paper stuck together with sticky tape, I would have, but we weren't allowed to fiddle round too much with the enlarger.

I moved the focusing knob to get a sharp image but nothing much happened. The negative just wouldn't come into focus. I tried all the others I'd taken, then realised with humiliation that it was because I hadn't got the distances right in the first place when I took the photos.

"Very well, then," I thought. "It will be an artistically blurry photograph. Anyone can take an ordinary, focused picture. Mine will be original and different."

I used up quite a lot of paper making prints, but they didn't really look artistically blurred. They just looked like close ups of tree bark that hadn't been properly focused. However, I examined the biggest print under white light, and convinced myself that it was just like one of those big misty greeting cards you buy in shops. (Inside they have messages written in silver ink saying, "Serenity is footprints along a solitary shore" and they cost five weeks' pocket money.)

Several people were kicking down the door and yelling it was their turn and what was I taking so long over. I hid all the wasted pieces of paper so nobody would suspect I'd run into slight technical difficulties. Then I took the print out on a paper towel to show Miss Lattimore and Alison Ashley a thing or two. All the kids came crowding round to see if they were in it. They stared at my tree bark.

"What is it?" asked Margeart.

"Skin problems," said Sharlene.

"Leprosy," said Colin.

"Acne and blackheads," said Bill.

"Skin peeling off after a sunburn," said Lisa.

"Skin on a drowned corpse that's been in the water three months," said everyone.

"Don't be so disgusting," said Miss Lattimore. "At least Erica produced an entry for the competition, which is more than can be said for various other people in this grade. It's very nice, Yuk. A very nice print of . . . What exactly is it, Erica?"

Barry Hollis, back from being sorted out by Miss Belmont and Mr Nicholson, shoved his face up to my print and peered. "It's got a dirty word written on it," he said. "She's taken a picture of a dirty word."

"Barry Hollis, I have just about had enough of you," said Miss Lattimore sternly. "You spoil every class. You never want to learn. You're the rudest boy I ever met. You think you're being so smart, but you are just boring and tedious."

Barry Hollis had been hearing similar observations from every adult in his life, probably since the day he was born, so he wasn't offended or anything. He turned my photograph upside down and traced across it with his finger. "Take a look at that," he said.

I could have died.

There, carved in large scribbled letters deep into the bark of that tree, right on the section I'd photographed, was an obscene word. Everyone began to cheer and clap and stamp their feet.

"Fancy a tree knowing that word," said Margeart Collins dopily when Miss Lattimore quietened everyone down and was reaching in her handbag for a throat lozenge.

"I didn't notice it when I took that photo, or when I was doing the enlarging," I said. "I guess I had the negative in upside down. I didn't take a photo of a rude word on purpose, Miss Lattimore."

She gave me a very disappointed, suspicious look and didn't say anything.

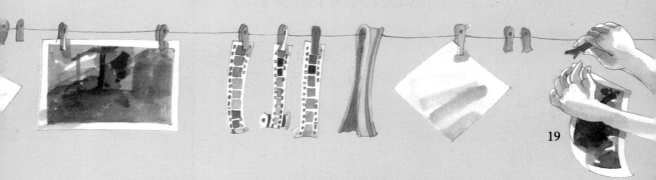

19

"I can still enter this print in the competition upside down, can't I?" I asked.

"Certainly not," said Miss Lattimore when the Strepsil had worked enough for her voice to come back. "It would give this school a bad name, a worse one than it has already, if any of the judges noticed. Alison's print can represent this grade from our school. And I wouldn't be at all surprised if it won a prize in its section."

Alison Ashley, I thought, I wish something terrible would happen to you! The elastic in your pants would bust, and you'd lose them somewhere really embarrassing and public, like Monday-morning assembly. Or you'd get into a busy lift, and somehow press a whole bunch of buttons at the same time, and make the lift get stuck for about six hours with a crowd of managing directors all on their way to important meetings, and they'd know you were responsible.

I went out the front to put my rude photo in the waste-paper bin.

She came right out behind me to sharpen a pencil. I searched her navy-blue eyes for emotions, but as usual you couldn't tell what Alison Ashley was thinking. I figured she must have been feeling what I would have, if I'd been in her position. Triumph.

"Pity about your photo," she said. "It certainly was original. It's a shame it has to end up in the bin after all your hard work."

Standing there batting her innocent, blue, kitten eyes and purring like a cat full of mouse. Gloating through every triumphant minute.

There is a limit to what a person can endure.

"You think you're better than anyone else in Barringa East Primary, Alison Ashley," I said furiously. "Stop acting so snobby and stuck up. And quit picking on people, too. You've got to be careful whom you pick on at this school."

"Who said I was picking on anyone?"

"Let me tell you, Alison Ashley," I said. "I have some very powerful friends in this school who don't like me being picked on. In school hours, or out of school hours."

"Congratulations," she said, and tapped the pencil shavings into the bin. Then she began to sharpen the pencil at the other end. (Which just showed what a mean, ungenerous nature she had.)

"So I'm just warning you, Alison Ashley," I said. "If you go on showing me up all the time in school and everywhere, then I'll have no other alternative."

"Than what?"

"Than to ask my best friend Barry Hollis to bash you up."

"Well then, why don't you ask him now, Yuk?" she said pleasantly. "He's standing right behind you."

Eavesdropping, with his ears sticking out like lilies. He was just in the process of reacting to what I'd said about him being my best friend. His mouth was ajar with fury, and his fist bunching up into an almighty punch.

Luckily the bell rang for afternoon recess. As I didn't feel like spending it in the playground with Barry Hollis looking so dangerous, I headed for the sick bay.

Written by Robin Klein
Illustrated by Donna Gynall

R · E · V · E · N · G · E · !

I hate you, I hate you, I hate you, Anne Scully!
I hope a gorilla traps you in a gully!
Here are some curses I'm putting on you:
Measles at Christmas; at Easter, the 'flu;
That you don't have a ticket, and meet an inspector,
Who'll shove you right off with a blistering lecture.
I hope that at ballet, when up on your toes,
You look down and find out you're wearing no clothes.
And if Royalty asks you to dinner, you twerp,
I hope you spill gravy and then loudly burp.
When you go swimming, I hope a large creature,
With ten metre molars pops up to eatcha!
And in your lunchbox, instead of cake,
I hope you discover a copperhead snake!
You want to know why? Just listen then, smarty!
I WASN'T INVITED TO YOUR BIRTHDAY PARTY!

Robin Klein

23

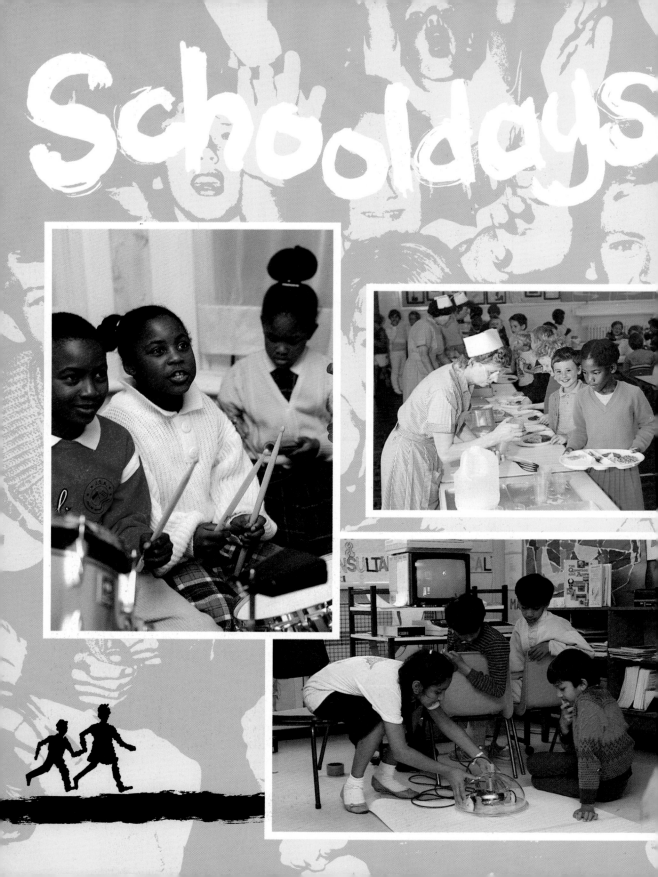

Schooldays

School days

Days

SUNDAY is a drowsy friend,
A miserable moaning day.
Monday is much the same,
You can't call it happy or gay.
Tuesday is a busy person,
A Day of work not talk.
Wednesday is worried and noisy
It is not a day for a peaceful walk.
Thursday is a person of changing mood,
It's a sort of mixed day.
Friday should be a happy friend
A happy, joyful day.
Saturday — here it comes!
Always happy, always full of fun!

Lucy Bassett
aged 12

Outside at Lunchtime

DO you know what it is like
To be outside at dinner time?
It is cold.
But they don't care.

They are warm.
We can see them with cups of tea.
But they don't know what it's like
To be out at dinnertime.

We know that some of us
Run in the corridors,
But it is cold and snowing
So let us in please.

Some of us had put chairs in the corridors,
Others had sandwiches in the classrooms.
But it is cold
So let us in please.

Some of us congregate in toilets
And in the corridors.
But please let us in.
Please, please, please.

Tina Clarke
aged 12

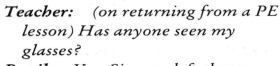

HEY! HEARD THIS ONE?

Teacher: (on returning from a PE lesson) Has anyone seen my glasses?

Pupil: Yes, Sir, you left them outside.

Teacher: Silly boy, why didn't you give them to me?

Pupil: I don't think you'd want them after I'd stepped on them!

Why did Cinderella get thrown out of the soccer team?
Because she kept running away from the ball.

Why did the teacher put on the lights?
Because the class was so dim.

Father: Do you want any help with your homework?

Daughter: No thanks, Dad, I'll get it wrong on my own.

Boy: My teacher does bird imitations.

Mum: Really?

Boy: She watches me like a hawk.

Teacher! Teacher! I've just swallowed my mouth organ. Think yourself lucky that you don't play the piano.

Teacher: Marie, did you miss maths today?

Marie: No, Miss, not a bit.

Have you read 'Fun and Puzzles' by Sarah Waytodoit?

No but I've read 'Did He do it?' by Betty Didunt.

Roses are red,
Violets are blue,
I copied your test
And I failed too!

Teacher: Do you want a pocket calculator?
Pupil: No, thank you, I know how many pockets I've got.

Teacher: Give me a sentence with the words defence, defeat and detail in it.
Sushi: When a horse jumps over defence, defeat go before detail.

Teacher: If you had five sweets on your desk and the boy next to you took three, what would you have?
Girl: A fight, Miss.

Jono: Miss, I ain't got a pencil.
Teacher: No, Jono, not ain't. I haven't got a pencil! They haven't got a pencil! You haven't got a pencil!
Jono: Wow! What happened to all the pencils?

Pupil: I don't think I deserved the O you gave me on my test.
Teacher: Neither do I, but it's the lowest I could give you.

What did the teacher say to the skeleton?
I've got a bone to pick with you.

CRAZY DEFINITIONS

BUOYANT
~ a male ant ~

FRIEND
~ someone who has the same enemies as you! ~

STREAKY BACON
~ a pig with no clothes on ~

31

DEAD GOOD

Geography is good, dead good,
there's maps to draw and colour,
better than writing essays, poems,
spellings and comprehensions,
yes, Geography is good, tracing and
outlining, different colours,
brown for mountains,
green for fields, blue for sea,
easy isn't it, no vexing verbs or
nasty nouns, thinking of adjectives,
or putting commas in the right place—
I think I could do Geography all day,
except for Games, that is, Games is good,
dead good, specially football...

Bill Boyle

BEG, BORROW OR...

Can I borrow ?

a rubber
a coloured pencil
a ruler
a biro

Can I borrow ?

a sports shirt
spare training shoes
a painting shirt
any felt pens

Can I borrow ?

someone's dinner
two left feet
three umbrellas
four pairs of gloves
five French books
six spelling bees
seven swimming lessons
eight elastic bands
nine Norman conquerors
ten tons of toffee ...
and the school caretaker
makes a lovely cup of tea.

Bill Boyle

May Day

When is it?

The first day of May.

Why is it celebrated and by whom?

It all depends on where you live. In many European countries it is a festival of spring and as such is a custom that goes way, way back to early pagan times. Young people used to go out into the fields on the first of May to dance and sing in honour of Flora, goddess of fruits and flowers.

In many areas the pine tree, which was considered sacred, became a part of the celebration. In England, people went out early on the first morning in May to cut down a tall young tree. They would lop off most of its branches, decorate it with flowers and ribbons and bring it back to the village green. There it would be set up as a focal point for their dancing and it was called the "Maypole".

Girls sometimes used to gather dew early on May Day, for it was believed that if you washed your face in May dew it would make you beautiful as well as bring you luck for the next twelve months. People also collected branches of hawthorn (which is also called May, because this is when it flowers) and made posies of spring flowers to carry or with which to decorate their houses. Fetes and festivals were held and people were chosen to be King and Queen of the May celebrations. For a time, during the 14th century, May Day become known as Robin Hood's Day in parts of England and a man and a woman were chosen to represent Robin and Maid Marion, and were called the Lord and Lady of the May.

In certain Greek villages still, the month of May is represented by a May boy. He wears a wreath of flowers and is escorted by a chorus of masked villagers as he dances through the streets singing May songs.

But there's another kind of May Day in many parts of the world. It's known as *International Labour Day* and is celebrated as a day to honour working people. There are marches and parades through city streets.

May Day is especially important in communist countries such as the USSR and China. Huge crowds gather for the celebrations and there are magnificent demonstrations of marching and dancing, especially by children. There is usually a parade of military weapons and personnel and it is seen as a day for rejoicing in the strength and solidarity of the nation.

Send Three and Fourpence We are Going to a Dance

Mike and Ruth Dixon got on well enough, but not so well that they wanted to walk home from school together. Ruth would not have minded, but Mike, who was two classes up, preferred to amble along with his friends so that he usually arrived a long while after Ruth did.

Ruth was leaning out of the kitchen window when he came in through the side gate, kicking a brick.

"I've got a message for you," said Mike. "From school. Miss Middleton wants you to go and see her tomorrow before assembly, and take a dead frog."

"What's she want *me* to take a dead frog for?" said Ruth. "She's not my teacher. I haven't got a dead frog."

"How should I know?" Mike let himself in. "Where's Mum?"

"Round Mrs Todd's. Did she really say a dead frog? I mean, really say it?"

"Derek told me to tell you. It's nothing to do with me."

Ruth cried easily. She cried now. "I bet she never. You're pulling my leg."

"I'm not, and you'd better do it. She said it was important — Derek said — and you know what a rotten old temper she's got," said Mike, feelingly.

"But why me? It's not fair." Ruth leaned her head on the window-sill and wept in earnest. "Where'm I going to find a dead frog?"

"Well, you can peel them off the road sometimes when they've been run over. They go all dry and flat, like pressed flowers," said Mike. He did think it a trifle unreasonable to demand dead frogs from little girls, but Miss Middleton *was* unreasonable. Everyone knew that. "You could start a pressed frog collection," he said.

Ruth sniffed fruitily. "What do you think Miss'll do if I don't get one?"

"She'll go barmy, that's what," said Mike. "She's barmy anyway," he said. "Nah, don't start howling again. Look, I'll go down the ponds after tea. I know there's frogs there because I saw the spawn, back at Easter."

"But those frogs are alive. She wants a dead one."

"I dunno. Perhaps we could get it put to sleep or something, like Mrs Todd's Tibby was. And don't tell Mum. She doesn't like me down the ponds and she won't let us have frogs indoors. Get an old box with a lid and leave it on the rockery, and I'll put old Froggo in it when I come home. *And stop crying!*"

After Mike had gone out Ruth found the box that her summer sandals had come in. She poked air holes in the top and furnished it with damp grass and a tin lid full of water. Then she left it on the rockery with a length of darning wool so that Froggo could be fastened down safely until morning. It was only possible to imagine Froggo alive; all tender and green and saying croak-croak. She could not think of him dead and flat and handed over to Miss Middleton, who definitely must have gone barmy. Perhaps Mike or Derek had been wrong about the dead part. She hoped they had.

37

She was in the bathroom, getting ready for bed, when Mike came home. He looked round the door and stuck up his thumbs.

"Operation Frog successful. Over and out."

"Wait. Is he . . . alive?"

"Shhh. Mum's in the hall. Yes."

"What's he like?"

"Sort of frog-shaped. Look, I've got him; OK? I'm going down now."

"Is he green?"

"No. More like that pork pie that went mouldy on top. Good night!"

Mike had hidden Froggo's dungeon under the front hedge, so all Ruth had to do next morning was scoop it up as she went out of the gate. Mike had left earlier with his friends, so she paused for a moment to introduce herself. She tapped quietly on the lid. "Hullo?"

There was no answering cry of croak-croak. Perhaps he *was* dead. Ruth felt a tear coming and raised the lid a fraction at one end. There was a scrabbling noise and at the other end of the box she saw something small and alive, crouching in the grass.

"Poor Froggo," she whispered through the air holes. "I won't let her kill you, I promise," and she continued on her way to school feeling brave and desperate, and ready to protect Froggo's life at the cost of her own.

The school hall was in the middle of the building and classrooms opened off it. Miss Middleton had Class 3 this year, next to the cloakroom. Ruth hung up her blazer, untied the wool from Froggo's box, and went to meet her doom. Miss Middleton was arranging little stones in an aquarium on top of the bookcase, and jerked her head when Ruth knocked, to show that she should come in.

"I got him, Miss," said Ruth, holding out the shoe box in trembling hands.

"What, dear?" said Miss Middleton, up to her wrists in water-weed.

"Only he's not dead and I won't let you kill him!" Ruth cried, and swept off the lid with a dramatic flourish. Froggo, who must have been waiting for this, sprung out, towards Miss Middleton, landed with a clammy sound on that vulnerable place between the collar bones, and slithered down inside Miss Middleton's blouse.

Miss Middleton taught Nature Study. She was not afraid of little damp creatures, but she was not expecting Froggo. She gave a squawk of alarm and jumped backwards. The aquarium skidded in the opposite direction; took off; shattered against a desk. The contents broke over Ruth's new sandals in a tidal wave, and Lily the goldfish thrashed about in a shallow puddle on the floor. People came running with mops and dustpans. Lily Fish was taken out by the tail to recover in the cloakroom sink. Froggo was arrested while trying to leave Miss Middleton's blouse through the gap between two buttons, and put back in his box with a weight on top in case he made another dash for freedom.

Ruth, crying harder than she had ever done in her life, was sent to stand outside the Headmaster's room, accused of playing stupid practical jokes; and cruelty to frogs.

Sir looked rather as if he had been laughing, but it seemed unlikely, under the circumstances, and Ruth's eyes were so swollen and tear-filled that she couldn't see clearly. He gave her a few minutes to dry out and then said, "This isn't like you, Ruth. Whatever possessed you to go throwing frogs at poor Miss Middleton? And poor frog, come to that."

"She told me to bring her a frog," said Ruth, stanching another tear at the injustice of it all. "Only she wanted a dead one, and I couldn't find a dead one, and I couldn't kill Froggo. I won't kill him," she said, remembering her vow on the way to school.

"Miss Middleton says she did not ask you to bring her a frog, or kill her a frog. She thinks you've been very foolish and unkind," said Sir, "and I think you are not telling the truth. Now . . . "

"Mike told me to," said Ruth.

"Your brother? Oh, come now."

"He did. He said Miss Middleton wanted me to go to her before assembly with a dead frog and I did, only it wasn't dead and I won't!"

"Ruth! Don't grizzle. No one is going to murder your frog, but we must get this nonsense sorted out." Sir opened his door and called to a passer-by, "Tell Michael Dixon that I want to see him at once, in my office."

Mike arrived, looking wary. He had heard the crash and kept out of the way, but a summons from Sir was not to be ignored.

"Come in, Michael," said Sir. "Now, why did you tell your sister that Miss Middleton wanted her to bring a dead frog to school?"

"It wasn't me," said Mike. "It was a message from Miss Middleton."

"Miss Middleton told you?"

"No, Derek Bingham told me. She told him to tell me — I suppose," said Mike, sulkily. He scowled at Ruth. All her fault.

"Then you'd better fetch Derek Bingham here right away. We're going to get to the bottom of this."

Derek arrived. He too had heard the crash.

"Come in, Derek," said Sir. "I understand that you told Michael here some tarradiddle about his sister. You let him think it was a message from Miss Middleton, didn't you?"

"Yes, well . . ." Derek shuffled. "Miss Middleton didn't tell *me*. She told, er, someone, and they told me."

"Who was this someone?"

Derek turned all noble and stood up straight and pale. "I can't remember, Sir."

"Don't let's have any heroics about sneaking, Derek, or I shall get very *cross*."

Derek's nobility ebbed rapidly. "It was Tim Hancock, Sir. He said Miss Middleton wanted Ruth Dixon to bring her a dead dog before assembly."

"A dead *dog*?"

"Yes, Sir."

"Didn't you think it a bit strange that Miss Middleton should ask Ruth for a dead dog, Derek?"

"I thought she must have one, Sir."

"But why should Miss Middleton want it?"

41

"Well, she does do Nature Study," said Derek.

"Go and fetch Tim," said Sir.

Tim had been playing football on the field when the aquarium went down. He came in with an innocent smile which wilted when he saw what was waiting for him.

"Sir?"

"Would you mind repeating the message that you gave Derek yesterday afternoon?"

"I told him Miss Middleton wanted Sue Nixon to bring her a red sock before assembly," said Tim. "It was important."

"Red sock? Sue Nixon?" said Sir. He was beginning to look slightly wild-eyed. "Who's Sue Nixon? There's no one in this school called Sue Nixon."

"I don't know any of the girls, Sir," said Tim.

"Didn't you think a red sock was an odd thing to ask for?"

"I thought she was bats, Sir."

"Sue Nixon?"

"No, Sir. Miss Middleton, Sir," said truthful Tim.

Sir raised his eyebrows. "But why did you tell Derek?"

"I couldn't find anyone else, Sir. It was late."

"But why Derek?"

"I had to tell someone or I'd have got into trouble," said Tim, virtuously.

"You are in trouble," said Sir. "Michael, ask Miss Middleton to step in here for a moment, please."

Miss Middleton, frog-ridden, looked round the door.

"I'm sorry to bother you again," said Sir, "but it seems that Tim thinks you told him that one Sue Nixon was to bring you a red sock before assembly."

"Tim!" said Miss Middleton, very shocked. "That's a naughty fib. I never told you any such thing."

"Oh Sir," said Tim. "Miss didn't tell me. It was Pauline Bates done that."

"*Did* that. I think I see Pauline out in the hall," said Sir. "In the PT class. Yes? Let's have her in."

Pauline was very small and very frightened. Sir sat her on his knee and told her not to worry. "All we want to know," he said, "is what you said to Tim yesterday. About Sue Nixon and the dead dog."

"Red sock, Sir," said Tim.

"Sorry. Red sock. Well, Pauline?"

Pauline looked as if she might join Ruth in tears. Ruth had just realised that she was no longer involved, and was crying with relief.

"You said Miss Middleton gave you a message for Sue Nixon. What was it?"

"It wasn't Sue Nixon," said Pauline, damply. "It was June Nichols. It wasn't Miss Middleton, it was Miss Wimbledon."

"There *is* no Miss Wimbledon," said Sir. "June Nichols, yes. I know June, but Miss Wimbledon . . . ?"

"She means Miss Wimpole, Sir," said Tim. "The big girls call her Wimbledon 'cause she plays tennis, Sir, in a little skirt."

"I thought you didn't know any girls," said Sir. "What did Miss Wimpole say to you, Pauline?"

"She didn't," said Pauline. "It was Moira Thatcher. She said to tell June Nichols to come and see Miss Whatsit before assembly and bring her bed socks."

"Then why tell Tim?"

"I couldn't find June. June's in his class."

"I begin to see daylight," said Sir. "Not much, but it's there. All right, Pauline. Go and get Moira, please."

Moira had recently had a new brace fitted across her front teeth. It caught the light when she opened her mouth.

"Yeth, Thir?"

"Moira, take it slowly, and tell us what the message was about June Nichols."

Moira took a deep breath and polished the brace with her tongue.

"Well, Thir, Mith Wimpole thaid to thell June to thee her before athembly with her wed fw — thw — thth — "

"Frock?" said Sir. Moira nodded gratefully. "So why tell Pauline?"

"Pauline liveth up her thtweet, Thir."

"No I don't," said Pauline. "They moved. They got a council house, up the Ridgeway."

"All right, Moira," said Sir. "Just ask Miss Wimpole if she could thp — spare me a minute of her time, please?"

If Miss Wimpole was surprised to find eight people in Sir's office, she didn't show it. As there was no longer room to get inside, she stood at the doorway and waved. Sir waved back. Mike instantly decided that Sir fancied Miss Wimpole.

"Miss Wimpole, I believe you must be the last link in the chain. Am I right in thinking that you wanted June Nichols to see you before assembly, with her red frock?"

44

"Why, yes," said Miss Wimpole. "She's dancing a solo at the end-of-term concert. I wanted her to practise, but she didn't turn up."

"Thank you," said Sir. "One day, when we both have a spare hour or two, I'll tell you why she didn't turn up. As for you lot," he said, turning to the mob round his desk, "you seem to have been playing 'Chinese Whispers' without knowing it. You also seem to think that the entire staff is off its head. You may be right. I don't know. Red socks, dead dogs, live frogs — we'll put your friend in the school pond, Ruth. Fetch him at break. And now, someone had better find June Nichols and deliver Miss Wimpole's message."

"Oh, there's no point, Sir. She couldn't have come anyway," said Ruth. "She's got chicken-pox. She hasn't been at school for ages."

by Jan Mark
Illustrated by Maria Yeap

In the story you have just read, Miss Wimpole gave Moira Thatcher a message. Moira passed it to Pauline Bates, who passed it on to Tim Hancock, who passed it on to Derek Bingham, who told Mike Dixon, and Mike told his sister Ruth. The message, "to bring a red frock to school", which should have been given to June Nichols, became "bring a dead frog to school" and was given to Ruth Dixon!

The title "Send Three and Fourpence, we are Going to a Dance" comes from an old story about a battle. Radio communications had broken down and so the officer-in-charge asked that a message be whispered from soldier to soldier back to headquarters. The officer's message was: "Send reinforcements we are going to advance". What do you think was the message received by headquarters?!

Passing messages to see how garbled they can become has been turned into a party game called "Chinese Whispers". Why it's *Chinese* Whispers, no one seems to know!

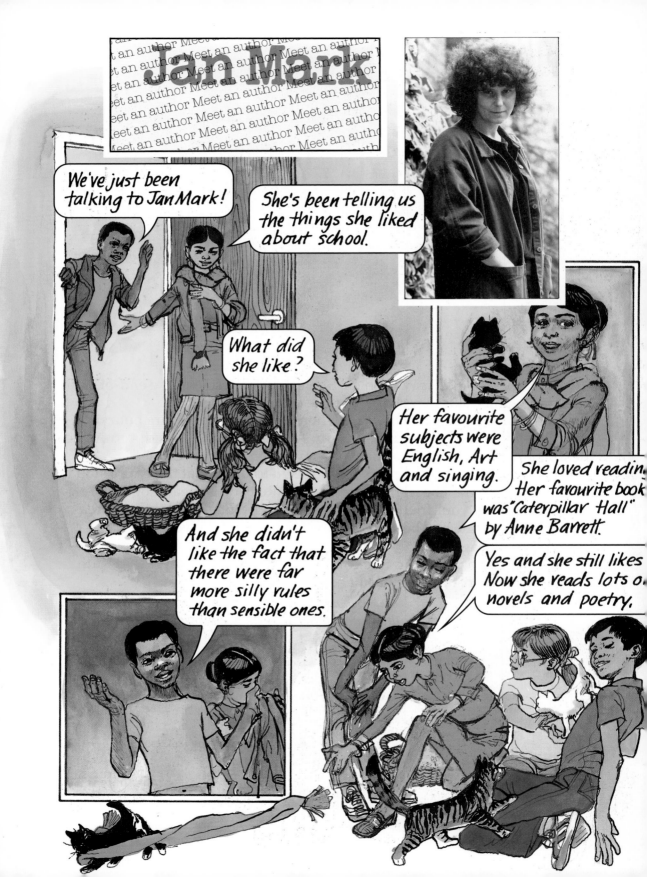

Excuses for Being Late

If you are ever late for school, it is more than likely that your teacher will demand some explanation (spoil-sport!). If you do not have a reasonable excuse try one of the following:

I broke my ankle (rather a lame excuse).

I squeezed my toothpaste too hard and it took me ages to get it back into the tube.

You rang the bell before I got here.

I must have over-washed.

There was a notice on my bus saying, "Dogs Must Be Carried" and it took me ages to find one.

Last night I dreamt about a football match and it went into extra time, so I stayed asleep to see the finish.

There are only seven people in our house but the alarm clock was set for eight.

There's a sign outside that says "School Ahead — Go Slow", so I obeyed it.

Peter Eldin

THE IDEAL SCHOOL TIME TABLE!

	DAY OF REST AFTER LOVELY WEEKEND	TUESDAY	WEDNESDAY	THURSDAY	DAY OF PREPARATION FOR LOVELY WEEKEND
9.00 am	Private limousine will pick you up. Breakfast is served on board.	Free choice activities: popcorn making, clay modelling, sports, yoga, giggling, guitar playing.	Helicopter trip to Luna Park.	School trip to beach to discover how waves work on hot sunny days. (If wet, a trip to chocolate factory.)	Waxing skateboards.
9.15					
9.30	School starts at 10.00 am on Mondays! Free choice activities: money making, eating, bubblegum blowing, photography, etymology, acting, snorkelling, painting, yodelling.				
9.45					
10.00 am	Morning recess: Teachers provide scones, jam and cream for you in staffroom.				
10.15		Water slide work out.	Read jokes and riddles. Practise juggling.	Learn to play drums. Learn magic tricks.	Science: find out how to control weather. Plan trip to disperse clouds.
10.30					
10.45					
11.00 am	Extra long lunch breaks, so you have time to enjoy free fish and chip lunches organised by your school tuck-shop; TV viewing; skateboard championships; cloud gazing etc.				
1.00 pm	Better do a bit of maths.	Watch Star Wars on the video.	Free choice activities: more eating, singing, chasing, space travel, gymnastics, dancing, treasure hunt, horse rides.	Play computer games.	Watch Return of The Jedi on video.
1.15	Lolly scramble.			Try jogging.	
1.30	Better do a bit of spelling.			Attack a crossword puzzle.	
1.45	Skateboard practice.			Afternoon snooze.	
2.00 pm		Learning to read backwards.			School finishes at 2.00 pm. Skateboard home for a lovely long weekend.
2.15	Swimming.	Let off steam in school hall run and scream.	Painting murals on school buildings.	Free choice activities: ice skating, face painting, fishing, hot-air balloon rides, cooking, stamp collecting.	
2.30					
2.45		Better write something.			
3.00 pm					

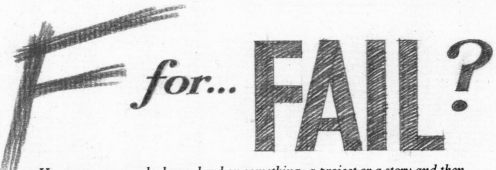

F for... FAIL?

Have you ever worked very hard on something, a project or a story and then found that nobody, not even the teacher thought it was any good?
Does it still happen?

In this story Anastasia, who is only in fourth grade, is about to find out how it feels . . .

Anastasia Krupnik was ten. She had hair the colour of Hubbard squash, fourteen freckles across her nose (and seven others in places that she preferred people not to know about), and glasses with large owl-eyed rims, which she had chosen herself at the optician's.

Once she had thought that she might like to be a professional ice skater. But after two years of trying, she still skated on the insides of her ankles.

Once she had thought that she might like to be a ballerina, but after a year of Saturday morning ballet lessons, she still couldn't get the fifth position exactly right.

Her parents said, very kindly, that perhaps she should choose a profession that didn't involve her feet. She thought that probably they were right, and she was still trying to think of one.

Anastasia had a small pink wart in the middle of her left thumb. She found her wart very pleasing. It had appeared quite by surprise, shortly after her tenth birthday, on a morning when nothing else interesting was happening, and it was the first wart she had ever had, or even seen.

"It's the loveliest colour I've ever seen in a wart," her mother, who had seen others, said with admiration.

"Warts, you know," her father had told her, "have a kind of magic to them. They come and go without any reason at all, rather like elves."

Anastasia's father, Dr Myron Krupnik, was a professor of literature and had read just about every book in the world, which may have been why he knew so much about warts. He had a beard the colour of Hubbard squash, though not much hair on his head, and he wore glasses for astigmatism, as Anastasia did, although his were not quite as owly. He was also a poet. Sometimes he read his poems to Anastasia by candlelight, and let her take an occasional (very small) sip of his wine.

Katherine Krupnik, her mother, was a painter. Very often there was a smudge of purple on her cheek, or a daub of green on one wrist or elbow. Sometimes she smelled of turpentine, which painters use; sometimes she smelled of vanilla and brown sugar, which mothers use; and sometimes, not very often, she smelled of Je Reviens perfume.

In the bookcases of their apartment were four volumes of poetry which had been written by Myron Krupnik. The first one was called *Laughter Behind the Mask*, and on the back of the book was a photograph of Myron Krupnik, much younger, when he had a lot of hair, holding his glasses in one hand and half-smiling as if he knew a secret. Anastasia's father hated that book, or said that he did. Anastasia sometimes wondered why he kept it in the bookcase if he hated it so much. She thought it must be a little like the feeling she had had when she was eight, when she hated a boy named Michael McGuire so much that she walked past his house every day, just to stick out her tongue.

The second book of poetry by her father had a photograph of him with slightly less hair and a mustache; it was called *Mystery of Myth*. Her father liked it. But her mother didn't like it at all. The reason her mother didn't like it at all was because on one of the inside front pages it said, "For Annie". Anastasia didn't know who Annie was. She suspected that her mother did.

The third book was her mother's favourite, probably because *it* said, inside, "For Katherine". It was called *Come Morning, Come Night* and was filled with love poems that Anastasia found very embarrassing.

But the fourth book was her favourite. Her father's photograph showed him bald and bearded, the way she had always known him. The poems were soft sounding and quiet, when he read them to her. The book was called *Bittersweet*; and it said, inside, "To someone special: Anastasia".

Sometimes, when no one was in the room, Anastasia took *Bittersweet* down from the shelf, just to look at that page. Looking at it made her feel awed, unique, and proud.

Awed, unique, and *proud* were three words that she had written on page seven of her green notebook. She kept lists of her favourite words; she kept important private information; and she kept things that she thought might be the beginnings of poems, in her green notebook. No one had ever looked inside the green notebook except Anastasia.

On page one, the green notebook said, "My name is Anastasia Krupnik. This is the year that I am ten".

On page two, it said, "These are the most important things that happened the year that I was ten".

So far, there were only two things on the list. One was, "I got a small pink wart". And the other was, "My teacher's name is Mrs. Westvessel".

Mrs Westvessel wore stockings with seams up the back, and shoes that laced on the sides. Sometimes, while she sat at her desk, she unlaced her shoes when she thought no one was watching, and rubbed her feet against each other. Under the stockings, on the tops of her toes, were tiny round things like small doughnuts.

Anastasia described the toe doughnuts to her mother, and her mother nodded and explained that those were called corn pads.

Anastasia wrote "corn pads" on page twenty-seven of her notebook.

Mrs Westvessel also had interesting brown spots on the backs of her hands, very large and lop-sided bosoms, and a faint gray mustache.

"I think Mrs Westvessel is probably over one hundred years old," Anastasia told her parents at dinner. "Probably about one hundred and twenty."

"Nobody lives to be one hundred and twenty," said her mother as she poured some mushroom gravy over Anastasia's meat loaf. "Unless they're in Tibet."

Her father wrinkled his forehead. "Perhaps Mrs Westvessel is a mutant," he said.

"Yes," agreed Anastasia. "Mrs Westvessel is a mutant, I believe."

Later she wrote "mutant" on page twenty-seven, under "corn pads". Anastasia was a very good speller; she sounded out the syllables of "mutant" correctly on the first try.

Anastasia didn't like Mrs Westvessel very much. That made her feel funny, because she had always liked — sometimes even loved — her teachers before.

So she wrote in her green notebook, "Why don't I like Mrs Westvessel?" and began to make a list of reasons. Making lists of reasons was sometimes a good way to figure things out.

"*Reason one*:" wrote Anastasia, "Because she isn't a good teacher".

But then she crossed out reason one, because it was a lie. Anastasia wasn't crazy about telling lies, even to herself; she did it, sometimes, but it always gave her a stomach-ache.

Mrs Westvessel, she knew, was really a pretty good teacher. At any rate, she had taught Anastasia to remember the difference between minuends and subtrahends, which was not a particularly interesting thing to know; and also how to say "I love you" in both French and German, which was not only very interesting but might come in handy someday.

"*Reason two*:" wrote Anastasia, after she had crossed out reason *one*, "Because she is so old".

That wasn't a lie, so it didn't give her a stomach-ache; but it was a reason that Anastasia felt a little strange about. Anastasia felt a little strange about old people in general. Probably it was because of her grandmother, who was the oldest person she knew. Her grandmother was so old that she lived in a nursing home; and Anastasia didn't like to visit her there. The nursing home smelled of medicine and Polident, a bad combination of smells.

But Mrs Westvessel smelled of chalk dust and Elmer's Glue, which was not a bad combination at all. And Mrs Westvessel, although she was old, never *acted* old. When they were studying Ireland in geography, Mrs Westvessel had done an Irish jig in her laced-up shoes, with her bosoms bouncing. *That*, thought Anastasia, wasn't an *old* thing to do.

So she slowly crossed out reason *two*. Then she couldn't think of any others. Finally she wrote, "*Reason three*: Because I am dumb".

Not dumb in school. Anastasia, particularly after she had finally mastered the difference between minuends and subtrahends, was actually a very good student.

"I'm dumb," said Anastasia sadly to herself, "because sometimes — too many times — I don't feel the same way about things that everybody else feels".

"I was the only one at Jennifer MacCauley's birthday party," she remembered gloomily, "who thought green ice cream was nauseating. Everybody even *said* I was dumb, for that."

"I'm the only person in the world," she reminded herself, " — the whole entire world — who likes cold spinach sandwiches. That's really dumb."

"And now," she thought, "I'm the only kid in the fourth grade who doesn't like Mrs Westvessel."

So reason *three* seemed to be the reason. "Because I'm dumb." She left it there, frowned, and closed her green notebook. "Sometimes," she thought, "maybe it isn't a good idea after all to make a list and find out the answer to a question".

But when Mrs Westvessel announced one day in Autumn that the class would begin writing poetry, Anastasia was the happiest she had ever been in school.

Somewhere, off in a place beyond her own thoughts, Anastasia could hear Mrs Westvessel's voice. She was reading some poems to the class; she was talking about poetry and how it was made. But Anastasia wasn't really listening. She was listening instead to the words that were appearing in her own head, floating there and arranging themselves into groups, into lines, into poems.

There were so many poems being born in Anastasia's head that she ran all the way home from school to find a private place to write them down, the way her cat had once found a very private place — the pile of ironing in the pantry — in which to create kittens.

But she discovered that it wasn't easy. She hung the Do Not Disturb sign from the Parker House Hotel on the doorknob of her bedroom door. She thought that might make it easier.

She got herself a glass of orange juice with ice in it, to sip on while she worked. She thought that might make it easier.

She put on her Red Sox cap. She thought that might make it easier.

But it still wasn't easy at all. Sometimes the words she wrote down were the wrong words, and didn't say what she wanted them to say, didn't make the sounds that she wanted them to make. Soon her Snoopy wastebasket was filled with crumpled pages, crumpled beginnings of poems.

Her mother knocked on her bedroom door and called, "Anastasia? Are you all right?"

"Yes," she called back, taking her pencil eraser out of her mouth for a minute. "I'm writing a poem."

Her mother understood that, because very often Anastasia's father would close the door to his study when he was writing a poem, and wouldn't come out even for dinner. "Okay, love," her mother said, the way she said it to Anastasia's father.

It took her eight evenings to write one poem. Even then, she was surprised when she realised that it was finished. She read it aloud, alone in her room, behind the Do Not Disturb sign from the Parker House Hotel; and then she read it aloud again, and smiled.

Then she read it aloud one more time, put it into the top drawer of her desk, took out her green notebook, and added to the list on page two under "These are the most important things that happened the year that I was ten," as item three: "I wrote a wonderful poem".

Then she flipped the Do Not Disturb sign on her doorknob to its opposite side, the side her mother didn't like. "Maid," said the opposite side, "please make up this room as soon as possible".

Her poem was finished just in time for Creativity Week.

Mrs Westvessel was very, very fond of Weeks. In their class, already this year, they had had Be Kind to Animals Week, when the bulletin board had been filled with newspaper clippings about dogs who had found lost children in deep woods, cats that had travelled three hundred miles home after being left behind in strange cities, and a cow in New Hampshire that had been spray-painted red during hunting season so that she would not be mistaken for a deer.

During My Neighbourhood Week, one entire classroom wall had been covered with paper on which they had made a mural: each child had drawn a building to create My Neighbourhood. There were three Luigi's Pizzas; two movie theatres, both showing *Superman*; one Red Sox Stadium; a split-level house with a horse tied to a tree in the yard; two Aquariums; two Science Museums; one Airport control tower; three State Prisons; and a condemned apartment building with a large rat on the front steps. Mrs Westvessel said that it was not what she had had in mind, and that next time she would give better instructions.

Creativity Week was the week that the fourth grade was to bring their poems to school. On Monday morning Mrs Westvessel took them on a field trip to Longfellow's home on Brattle Street. On Tuesday afternoon, a lady poet — poetess, she should be called, according to Mrs Westvessel; but the lady poet frowned and said she preferred poet, please — came to visit the class and read some of her poems. The lady poet wore dark glasses and had crimson fingernails. Anastasia didn't think that Longfellow would have liked the lady poet at all, *or* her poems.

Wednesday was the day that the members of the class were to read their own poems, aloud.

Robert Giannini stood in front of the class and read:

> *I have a dog whose name is Spot.*
> *He likes to eat and drink a lot.*
> *When I put water in his dish,*
> *He laps it up just like a fish.*

Anastasia hated Robert Giannini's poem. Also, she thought it was a lie. Robert Giannini's dog was named Sputnik; everyone in the neighbourhood knew that; and Sputnik had bitten two kids during the summer and if he bit one more person the police said the Gianninis would have to get rid of him.

But Mrs Westvessel cried, "Wonderful!" She gave Robert Giannini an A and hung his poem on the wall. Anastasia imagined that Longfellow was eyeing it with distaste.

Traci Beckwith got up from her desk, straightened her tights carefully, and read:

> *In autumn when the trees are brown,*
> *I like to walk all through the town.*
> *I like to see the birds fly south.*
> *Some have worms, still, in their mouths.*

Traci Beckwith blushed, and said, "It doesn't rhyme exactly".

"Well," said Mrs Westvessel, in a kind voice, "your next one will be better, I'm sure". She gave Traci Beckwith a B plus, and hung the poem on the wall next to Robert's.

Anastasia had begun to feel a little funny, as if she had ginger ale inside of her knees. But it was her turn. She stood up in front of the class and read her poem. Her voice was very small, because she was nervous.

> *hush   hush   the sea-soft night is aswim*
> > *with wrinklesquirm creatures*
> > > > *listen(!)*
> *to them   move   smooth   in the moistly dark*
> > *here in the   whisperwarm   wet*

That was Anastasia's poem.

"Read that again, please, Anastasia, in a bigger voice," said Mrs Westvessel.

So Anastasia took a deep breath and read her poem again. She used the same kind of voice that her father did when he read poetry to her, drawing some of the words out as long as licorice sticks, and making some others thumpingly short.

The class laughed.

Mrs Westvessel looked puzzled. "Let me see that, Anastasia," she said. Anastasia gave her the poem.

Mrs Westvessel's ordinary, everyday face had about one hundred wrinkles in it. When she looked at Anastasia's poem, her forehead and nose folded up so that she had two hundred new wrinkles all of a sudden.

"Where are your capital letters, Anastasia?" asked Mrs Westvessel.

Anastasia didn't say anything.

"Where is the rhyme?" asked Mrs Westvessel. "It doesn't rhyme at *all*."

Anastasia didn't say anything.

"What kind of poem *is* this, Anastasia?" asked Mrs Westvessel. "Can you explain it, please?"

Anastasia's voice had become very small again, the way voices do, sometimes. "It's a poem of sounds," she said. "It's about little things that live in tidepools, after dark, when they move around. It doesn't have sentences or capital letters because I wanted it to look on the page like small creatures moving in the dark."

"I don't know why it doesn't rhyme," she said, miserably. "It didn't seem important."

"Anastasia, weren't you *listening* in class when we talked about writing poems?"

Anastasia looked at the floor. "No," she whispered, finally.

Mrs Westvessel frowned, and rubbed her jiggly bosom thoughtfully. "Well," she said, at last.

"Well. Anastasia, when we talked about poetry in this class we simply were not talking about worms and snails crawling on a piece of paper. I'm afraid I will have to give you an F."

60

An F. Anastasia had never had an F in her entire life. She kept looking at the floor. Someone had stepped on a red crayon once; the colour was smeared into the wood forever.

"Iworkedveryhardonthatpoem," whispered Anastasia to the floor.

"Speak up, Anastasia."

Anastasia lifted her head and looked Mrs Westvessel in the eye. "I worked very, very hard on that poem," she said, in a loud, clear voice.

Mrs Westvessel looked terribly sad. "I can tell that you did, Anastasia," she said. "But the trouble is that you didn't listen to the instructions. I gave very, very careful instructions to the class about the kind of poems you were to write. And you were here that day; I remember that you were."

"Now if, in geography, I explained to the class just how to draw a map, and someone didn't listen, and drew his own kind of map" (everyone glanced at Robert Giannini, who blushed — he had drawn a beautiful map of Ireland, with cartoon figures of people throwing bombs all over it, and had gotten an F) "even though it was a very *beautiful* map, I would have to give that person a failing grade because he didn't follow the instructions. So I'm afraid I will have to do the same in this case, Anastasia."

"I'm sorry," said Mrs Westvessel.

"I just bet you are," thought Anastasia.

"If you work hard on another, perhaps it will be better. I'm *sure* it will be better," said Mrs Westvessel. She wrote a large F on the page of poetry, gave it back to Anastasia, and called on the next student.

At home, that evening, Anastasia got her green notebook out of her desk drawer. Solemnly, under "These are the most important things that happened the year that I was ten," in item three, she crossed out the word *wonderful* and replaced it with the word *terrible*.

"I wrote a terrible poem," she read sadly. Her goldfish, Frank, came to the side of his bowl and moved his mouth. Anastasia read his lips and said, "Blurp blurp blurp to you too, Frank".

Then she turned the pages of her notebook until she came to a blank one, page fourteen, and printed carefully at the top of the right-hand side: THINGS I HATE.

She thought very hard because she wanted it to be an honest list.

Finally she wrote down: "Mr Belden at the drugstore". Anastasia honestly hated Mr Belden, because he called her "girlie," and because once, in front of a whole group of fifth grade boys who were buying baseball cards, he had said the rottenest, rudest thing she could imagine anyone saying ever, and especially in front of a whole group of fifth grade boys. Mr Belden had said, "You want some Kover-up Kreme for those freckles, girlie?" And she had not been anywhere *near* the Kover-up Freckle Kreme, which was $1.39 and right between the Cuticura Soap and the Absorbine Jr.

Next, without any hesitation, Anastasia wrote down "Boys". She honestly hated boys. All of the fifth grade boys buying baseball cards that day had laughed.

"Liver" was also an honest thing. Everybody in the world hated liver except her parents.

And she wrote down "pumpkin pie," after some thought. She had *tried* to like pumpkin pie, but she honestly hated it.

And finally, Anastasia wrote, at the end of her THINGS I HATE list: "Mrs Westvessel". That was the most honest thing of all.

Then, to even off the page, she made a list on the left-hand side: THINGS I LOVE. For some reason it was an easier list to make.

Her parents were having coffee in the living room. "They're going to find out about the F when they go for a parent-teacher conference," thought Anastasia. "So I might as well show them." She took her poem to the living room. She held it casually behind her back.

"You guys know," she said, "how sometimes maybe someone is a great musician or something — well, maybe he plays the trumpet or something really well — and then maybe he has a kid, and it turns out the kid isn't any good at *all* at playing the trumpet?" Her parents looked puzzled.

"No," said her father. "What on earth are you talking about?"

She tried again. "Well, suppose a guy is a terrific basketball player. Maybe he plays for the Celtics and he's almost seven feet tall. Then maybe he has a kid, a little boy, and maybe the little boy *wants* to be a great basketball player. But he only grows to be five feet tall. So he can't be any good at basketball, right?"

"Is it a riddle, Anastasia?" her mother asked. "It seems very complicated."

"What if a man is a really good poet and his daughter tries to write a poem — I mean tries *really hard* — and the only poem she writes is a *terrible* poem?"

"Oh," said her father. "Let's see the poem, Anastasia."

Anastasia handed the poem to her father.

He read it once to himself. Then he read it aloud. He read it the way Anastasia had tried to, in class, so that some of the words sounded long and shuddery. When he came to the word "night" he said it in a voice as quiet as sleep. When he had finished, they were all silent for a moment. Her parents looked at each other.

"You know, Anastasia," her father said, finally. "Some people — actually, a *lot* of people — just don't understand poetry."

"It doesn't make them bad people," said her mother hastily.

"Just *dumb?*" suggested Anastasia. If she could change, under "Why don't I like Mrs Westvessel?" the answer "Because I'm dumb" to "Because *she's* dumb," maybe it wouldn't be such a discouraging question and answer after all.

But her father disagreed. "Not dumb," he said. "Maybe they just haven't been educated to understand poetry."

He took his red pen from his pocket. "I myself," he said grandly, "have been *very* well educated to understand poetry". With this red pen he added some letters to the F, so that the word *Fabulous* appeared across the top of the page.

Anastasia decided that when she went back to her room she would get her green notebook out again, and change page two once more. "I wrote a fabulous poem," it would say. She smiled.

"Daddy, do you think maybe someday I could be a poet?" she asked.

"Don't know why not," he said. "If you work hard at it."

Written by Lois Lowry
Illustrated by David Wong

BOTTOM OF THE CLASS

Are you the school dunce? If you are, don't worry about it. A lot of people who were bottom of the class went on to become famous.

The only thing Winston Churchill, the great statesman, got right in one Latin exam was his name.

Alfred Lord Tennyson, who became Poet Laureate in 1850, did not start to speak until he was four.

Before Isaac Newton became a great scientist he was bottom of the lowest form in the grammar school he attended.

Thomas Edison patented over a thousand inventions but at school he was always bottom.

Godfrey Housefield was not thought very bright at school but in 1979 he became joint winner of the Nobel Prize for Medicine.

One of Britain's greatest engineers, James Watt, was described by his teachers as "dull and inept".

Ten-year-old Albert Einstein was told by a teacher, "you will never amount to very much," and yet he became one of the world's greatest scientists.

When Henry Ford, founder of the Ford Motor Company, left school he had only a basic ability in reading and writing.

The great artist, Pablo Picasso, could hardly read or write when he was ten.

No ART in MATHS!

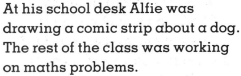

Alfie is another person who works hard . . . not at his school work but at his cartoons! His dream is that he'll be a cartoonist one day.

Alfie lives with his mum, his sister Alma, and Pap, his grandfather. His best friend is Tree (who got his nickname when he took the part of a weeping willow in a school play).

Alfie secretly thinks that his cartoons are touched with genius, but he is usually careful about showing them to anyone until . . .

At his school desk Alfie was drawing a comic strip about a dog. The rest of the class was working on maths problems.

Alfie had had the idea for his strip that morning during breakfast. Alma was talking about an article she'd read. "It said you shouldn't buy this kind of cereal, Mum."

"Why not?"

"Because it's got additives in it. Look on the box — artificial colouring, artificial flavouring — just read what we're eating."

Pap said, "It's better than hot dogs. There's rat hairs in them."

"Not at the table, please, Pap," Alfie's mother said.

"And where there's rat hairs, there's probably rat — "

"Pap!"

" — droppings."

"*Pap!*"

"Let *me* buy the cereal from now on, all right, Mum?" Alma said, getting up from the table.

Alfie was dipping his spoon into his soggy cereal, thinking up a comic strip about artificial flavouring.

"Alfie, are you going to sit there all morning or are you going to school?" his mum said finally.

"Don't bother me right now."

"Well, you're lucky to have somewhere to go, isn't he, Pap? Don't you wish you could go to school?"

"No."

Now Alfie had finished his comic strip. He had intended that as soon as he finished, he would begin work on his Maths problems, but now he sat admiring his work. His Maths was forgotten.

In the first square a large dog was reading the label on a can of dog food. "Artificial flavouring."

In the second square the dog was reading the label on a box of dog biscuits. "Artificial colouring."

In the third square the dog was reading the label on a dog collar. "Artificial fibres."

In the fourth square he was howling, "Is everything artificial these days?"

In the last square a little sign comes up from the dog's fur. "Fleas are still real!"

67

Alfie was very pleased with it. He wanted to take it up immediately and show it to his teacher, but she would know he had done it during Maths.

"All right," the teacher said, "time's up. Change papers with your partners and we'll check our work."

Alfie looked up, startled. He glanced at Tree. Dutifully Tree was holding out his paper to Alfie.

"Go easy," he said. He waited a minute with his hand outstretched and then he said, "Come on. Give me your paper." He snapped his fingers with impatience.

"I didn't do mine," Alfie whispered back, hiding his comic strip under his notebook.

"Why not?"

"I just didn't."

"But then I don't have anything to check!" Tree complained. He was upset. He loved to grade papers. It gave him a feeling of power. Grading papers made him want to become a teacher when he grew up.

"What's wrong back there, Tree?" Mrs Steinhart asked.

"Nothing."

"Alfie? Anything wrong?"

"No."

"All right then, we'll go over the first problem." Mrs Steinhart began to put the problem on the board. All the class bent over their papers.

Tree leaned forward too, hunched miserably over his bare desk. He shot Alfie a resentful look. Alfie did not glance at him. He was going over Tree's first problem.

Tree punched Alfie to get his attention. Then he acted out the difficulty of grading an invisible paper.

"Tree?" Mrs Steinhart called. He looked up.

"Is anything wrong?"

"What could be wrong, Mrs Steinhart?" This was what he always said when something was wrong that he was not free to discuss. He had got this from his sister, who had got it from soap operas.

"Whose paper are you grading?"

Tree looked down at his bare desk, the pencil in his hand. He sighed. "Alfie's."

"Bring it up here, please."

Tree's mouth fell open. He stared down at his desk. Finally he looked up at Mrs Steinhart. "I can't find his paper, Mrs Steinhart, that's what we were muttering about."

Alfie cleared his throat. "The reason he can't find my paper, Mrs Steinhart, is because I didn't do it. My mind was on something else."

"Oh." There was a pause, and then Mrs Steinhart said, "Well, then we'll continue without Alfie. Tree, give your paper to Maurice and you can grade Elizabeth's paper."

Tree's face lit up with delight. "Yes, *ma'am!*" He snatched his paper from Alfie and made the exchange. He took Elizabeth's paper with a flourish. "Revenge," he whispered happily. He pantomimed making big X's beside every one of her problems. "Is she going to be sorry she didn't take our picture yesterday!"

Alfie sat without moving. He thought about going up to Mrs Steinhart after class and explaining why he didn't do his Maths, but he knew he didn't have a good enough reason. Not comic strips. She wouldn't buy that. Maybe he could say he had an attack of something. He sat silent and miserable.

Tree punched him. "She missed number three," he whispered, his voice rising with delight, "subtracted instead of added".

He bent over Elizabeth's paper again, pencil poised for action. He began to whistle through his teeth. Alfie slumped lower in his desk.

Beside him Tree straightened abruptly. His hand shot into the air. "Oh, Mrs Steinhart," he called, "is that a two or a three on the second line?"

"It's a three." She went over the number with her chalk.

"That's what I was afraid of!" Tree said, singing the words in his joy. He made an elaborate X beside the problem. To Alfie he hissed, "She's missed two out of five. Bet she's really sorry she didn't take our picture!"

Alfie nodded by lowering his head. He lifted his notebook and glanced at his comic strip of the dog. He pulled it into view. It made him happy when one of his cartoons came out just right, but now he didn't smile.

Tree's long arm was waving in the air again. "Oh, Mrs Steinhart?"

She sighed. "Yes, Tree."

"How many can you miss and still pass?"

"This isn't a test, Tree."

"I know, but if it *was* a test?"

"Well, there are ten problems. Everyone should get at least seven, though I would like to see everyone have a perfect paper."

"Too late for *everyone* to get a perfect paper, Mrs Steinhart," Tree said cheerfully. Tree nudged Alfie. "If she misses one more she's — " He made a down gesture with his thumb.

Alfie nodded without enthusiasm. He took his comic strip and slipped it carefully in the back of his notebook in a pocket for special papers. When he got home he would put it up on the rafters in the attic. It deserved a place of honour, he thought, even though it couldn't cheer him up now.

Also in the pocket was a comic strip he had done the day before during English. He pulled it out and looked at it. "Super Giant."

In the first square the giant was destroying a forest, ripping trees from the earth, crying, "I love violence".

In the second square the giant was destroying a village. "I *love* violence!"

In the third square the giant was destroying a farm. "*I love violence!*"

In the last square the giant was flattened on the ground, being attacked by the villagers, the farm people, and the forest animals. He was saying, "It's things like this that take the fun out of violence".

The strip hadn't come out the way Alfie had wanted it to, and although he had spent most of English and Science trying to correct it, he had not succeeded. He saw now that he had failed because he had tried to put too much into each square. Perhaps if he . . .

Beside him Tree was desperately going over Elizabeth's paper one more time.

"Give me my paper, Tree," Elizabeth said. She tried to snatch it from him.

"In a minute, in a minute." He waved her away with his long arms. "I just want to make sure there aren't any more mistakes."

"Tree, give me my paper. Mrs Steinhart, Tree won't give me my paper."

"Tree."

"I'm just trying to be thorough, Mrs Steinhart, like you taught us. I know there's another mistake here. I just can't find it."

Elizabeth snatched her paper from him. "I'm rechecking this whole thing, Tree, and you better not have made any mistakes either."

"Me? Make mistakes?" Tree said. He looked as lofty as if he were in the forest, glancing down at a mere sapling. He took his own paper from Maurice. He fell silent.

"By the way, how many did *you* miss, Tree?" Elizabeth asked scornfully.

Tree didn't answer.

"All right, class," Mrs Steinhart said, "pass the papers to the front of the room, and, Alfie, I want to see you after school for a few minutes".

Alfie closed his notebook. He shook his hair out of his eyes. "Yes'm," he said.

"What'd she want?" Tree asked. He had been waiting for Alfie. He was leaning against the lone schoolground tree, his foot propped on a root. He seemed part of the landscape.

"Nothing," Alfie said.

A line of boys and girls were waiting to board the school bus. One of the boys called, "What'd she do to you, Alfie?"

"Nothing." He kept walking. All the grass had been worn off the schoolyard, and the dirt was packed as hard as concrete.

Tree fell into step with Alfie.

"What *did* she want?"

"If you *must* know — "

"I must."

" — she wanted to tell me I'm flunking Maths."

"That's supposed to be news?"

"Also she wants a conference with my mum."

"She must not know your mum."

Alfie kept walking, watching his feet.

"Nothing against your mum," Tree went on. "I just can't imagine anybody wanting to have a conference with her."

Alfie said nothing. He had made a terrible mistake in his talk with Mrs Steinhart, one he regretted deeply. In the middle of the talk, he had abruptly decided to take her into his confidence and show her his comic strip about the dog. This had been for two reasons. First, he really liked Mrs Steinhart, and, second, he did not want her to think he was just goofing off during Maths.

"Wait a minute," he had said.

He had hurried back to his desk and got his notebook. He had carried it to her, opened it, and carefully pulled out the comic strip. He had laid it before her like a fabric salesman.

"What's this, Alfie?" She put on her glasses.

"It's a comic strip, Mrs Steinhart. I drew it myself."

"This is what you were doing instead of your Maths problems?" she asked.

"Yes."

She looked at the strip. Alfie watched to see if a smile would come over her face. It did, but it was too faint to count. When she looked at Alfie the smile was gone. "You like to draw, don't you, Alfie, cartoons and things?"

"Yes."

"But —" She got even more serious. She took off her glasses. "But don't you think, Alfie, that there are times to draw — we do have Art, you know."

"I know," he said quickly. The week before they had cut out and coloured Indian symbols. School Art was as different from cartoons as Science was from recess.

Mrs Steinhart was still talking. "And then there are times for Maths and for English and for Science." She made it sound as exact as sorting mail.

He picked up his drawing and slid it back in the pocket of his notebook. "Yes."

"Your cartoon is really very good, and I think there's a lot of humour in it."

"Thank you."

"And you've made a good point about the way we live today. There *are* too many artificial things. I myself have started reading the labels on everything I buy."

"Thank you."

"Only you're going to have to do your cartoons after class."

"I know."

"I don't want to see you drawing again."

"You won't."

"Good." She smiled at him, a big smile now, the one he had wanted to see earlier when she had first looked at his comic strip. "You're a smart boy, Alfie, and I want you to do as well as I know you can."

"That's what I want too." He paused. "Can I go now?"

He had stumbled over his feet as he left the room. All the time he had been drawing his cartoons, he had secretly felt that they were touched with genius. He had known that if he had shared them with other people, they would have been as delighted as he. Now he *had* shown them — to his mother, Pap, Mrs Steinhart — and nothing had happened.

Written by Betsy Byars
Illustrated by Bettina Guthridge

ALFIE'S CARTOONS

Here are Alfie's cartoons from the previous story, re-drawn by PETER FOSTER.

Meet a cartoonist:
Peter Foster

Name: Peter Foster
Born at: Melbourne, Australia
Born on: May 18, 1931
Started school at: St. Mary's, Hampton
Favourite subjects at school: Art, Music, Gymnasium
What I didn't like about school: Chemistry

Favourite food when young: Roast Dinners

Favourite food now: Chinese Food

Best-loved story or book when young:
Kipling's "Jungle Book"

Favourite kind of books now: Art Books,
Music Books and
the Bible

Three things I love: Friends, Music and
Sundays (especially when all together)

Three things I hate: Rising early. Saying embarrassing things by accident. Sneezing while eating.

Secret wish: To conduct my own compositions.

Favourite riddle or joke: Any one that makes me cry
while I'm laughing.

Ethnic background: Australian
parents: English
grandparents: and Irish
Autograph: Foster

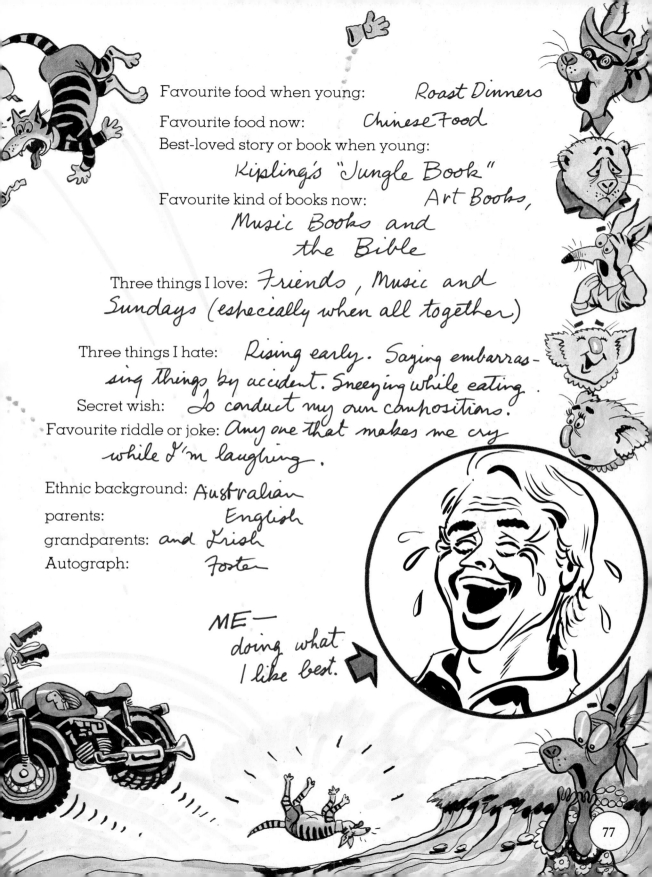

ME—
doing what
I like best.

A RECIPE FOR PAPER

1. Take some cloth rags, some old rope and a quantity of tree bark.
2. Soak well in water and beat until the fibres are well separated.
3. Put the pulpy mass into a mould and drain off the water.
4. Let the thin, felt-like material dry.

AND THERE'S YOUR PAPER!

That's the recipe that was invented nearly 2 000 years ago by a Chinese man named T'sai Lun. And basically it's still used today. *What gave him the idea?* Well, he didn't just wake up one morning and say, "I think I'll invent paper today". It doesn't happen that way. Most inventions are the result of hundreds of experiments that have gone before. Up till this time (AD 105), the main writing materials had been parchment (made from animal skins) and papyrus (an Egyptian invention, made from the stem of the papyrus plant). Papyrus was the most common in Egypt, Greece and Italy. The Chinese were interested in trying to find something that was cheaper and easier to handle than both these materials. 145 years earlier, another inventor named Meng T'ien had come up with the camel's hair brush, so during this time the Chinese had been experimenting with cloth for their scrolls and paintings. But no material was quite right, until along came T'sai Lun and his new paper.

The Chinese immediately decided to keep the recipe a secret from the rest of the world. But you know what happens to secrets!

 一言

來自

*That's Chinese for
"The name paper comes from the word papyrus".

MAKE YOUR OWN PAPER

- Ingredients:
  some paper towels
  brown paper bags and wrapping
  newspapers
  flower petals and blades of grass or
  vegetable colouring

- Utensils:
  3 baking trays (2 small, 1 large)
  a sponge or thick cloth
  1 deckle and 1 mould (see next page)
  1 blender

- Instructions:
  First tear the paper towels into little
  pieces, drop into a small baking tray,
  then cover with water.
  Next, tear up the brown paper bags, and do
  the same with them, using the other
  small tray.
  Leave for several days until you have a
  sloppy mush in each tray

Meanwhile, make your deckle and the mould. These need to be the same size and small enough to fit inside the large baking tray. Start by making 2 identical wooden frames small enough to fit inside your large baking tray. Leave one as it is. This is your deckle. Stretch and nail flyscreen wire on the other. It now becomes your mould.

Deckle

Wooden frames

Mould

Flyscreen wire

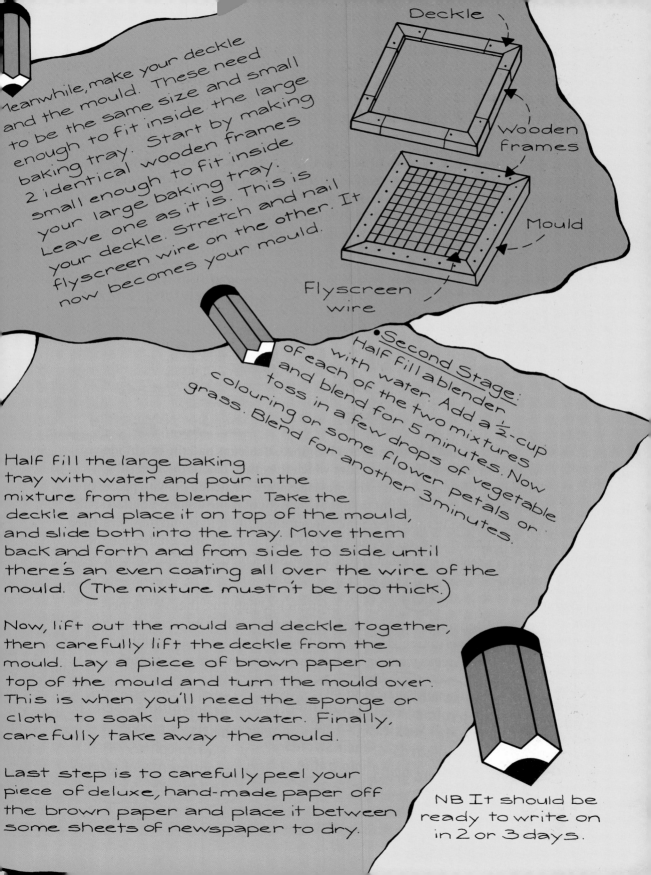

•Second Stage:
Half fill a blender with water. Add a ½-cup of each of the two mixtures and blend for 5 minutes. Now toss in a few drops of vegetable colouring or some flower petals or grass. Blend for another 3 minutes.

Half fill the large baking tray with water and pour in the mixture from the blender. Take the deckle and place it on top of the mould, and slide both into the tray. Move them back and forth and from side to side until there's an even coating all over the wire of the mould. (The mixture mustn't be too thick.)

Now, lift out the mould and deckle together, then carefully lift the deckle from the mould. Lay a piece of brown paper on top of the mould and turn the mould over. This is when you'll need the sponge or cloth to soak up the water. Finally, carefully take away the mould.

Last step is to carefully peel your piece of deluxe, hand-made paper off the brown paper and place it between some sheets of newspaper to dry.

NB It should be ready to write on in 2 or 3 days.

WHO INVENTED PENS?

Who knows? We'd be safe in saying people have always used their fingers to trace messages in sand or dirt, but there's no way of guessing who first thought to use a piece of burnt stick or charcoal to draw pictures on cave walls or which early artist first discovered that certain rocks and plants could be used to make coloured dyes or paint.

But some of it we can trace.

I wish your mother wouldn't write such long letters!

Around 3500 BC, the Chaldeans had the bright idea of writing on soft clay tablets or tiles which they then baked the way they baked their bricks. At first, the messages were scratched on with pieces of shell or broken pottery but then they thought of using a sharp pointed stick called a stylus. In time, someone had another bright idea and they scratched the letter characters on wedge-shaped bones and just pressed these in the clay. For really permanent records they used a metal stylus to write on stone pillars.

Once the Egyptians had papyrus, they developed a reed pen made from bullrushes or bamboo. Their ink came from a mixture of gall nuts (a tree growth caused by certain insects) and sulphate of iron. The Greeks went one better and got their ink from cuttlefish.

Roman soldiers often scratched their wills on their metal buckles or on the scabbards of their swords before going into battle.

The Egyptians used chisels to carve hieroglyphics on monuments of stone called obelisks.

...AND PENCILS?

Meanwhile, around 250 BC, the clever Chinese who'd been experimenting with brushes made from plants came up with the camel's-hair brush. Things were improving.

For everyone but camels.

And geese!

The quill pen came next, somewhere around the 13th century. It was made from a feather from the wing of a goose, the end being cut into a point with a small folding knife called a pen knife. (We still use this name today even though our pens no longer need sharpening.) Quills, together with ink made from soot or iron gall (from those gall nuts), were used all over the western world until the 1800s. Then in 1809, a Joseph Branah worked out that it would be cheaper to invent a permanent pen holder and just keep replacing the nib. He came up with a way of rapidly cutting quills into nibs. One more step forward!

I can't wait for the next stage.

Lots of people had been experimenting with pens made from horn and tortoiseshell, with pieces of diamond embedded in their points. The first steel pen and nib appeared in 1780, but it was too expensive for most folk and nothing much happened until 1820 when English inventor, James Perry produced a cheaper metal pen. Soon after, Josiah Mason invented a machine which made these pens so quickly and cheaply that everyone could own one.

(Everyone who could write, that is!)

Thank goodness! Thought they'd never get around to it.

I t was a long time before these pens found their way into schools, though. Popular school equipment right up till the beginning of the 20th century was the slate. Slates were made from thin pieces of rock set in wooden frames. The slate pencil (which was just a softer piece of slate shaped like a pencil) left a greyish-white mark on the darker rock and this could be wiped off with a damp rag — or saliva. Lots of kids got into trouble for spitting on their slates!

But of course they had pencils.

Wondered when you were getting around to us!

T he kind of pencil we know didn't turn up till around the 19th century. Before that, artists used silver wire fixed in a wooden holder. The parchment or paper had to be coated with a paste made from crushed bone or chalk mixed with water and gum or starch. Then the silverpoint, as it was called, was used on this. Very messy! And you couldn't rub out.

People using charcoal obviously decided that it would last longer if it was surrounded by wood (cleaner too!). The first modern-style pencil popped up around 1565 but it was 1785 before a Frenchman named Conte produced the first dependable lead pencil and much later before they were commonly used.

Somehow a graphite-and-clay pencil doesn't sound the same!

T he lead in a pencil isn't metal, by the way. It's a mixture of graphite (which is a form of carbon) and clay which is formed into paste, cut into lengths and baked at a high temperature until it's hard. The more graphite, the softer the pencil.

Colour pencils have a mixture of clay, wax and colouring matter instead of graphite.

Not a word about how rubbers come from trees!

Metal nib pens that had to be dipped into an ink well or bottle were used by everyone until the fountain pen became popular. The first practical fountain pen was made in 1884 by L. E. Waterhouse and had a metal lever that helped suck up the ink into a rubber tube inside the pen. (Lots of people had inky fingers those days and it was disastrous when you accidentally knocked over the bottle!)

But then they thought of cartridges and, of course, the biro appeared. This was invented by Hungarians, Lazlo and Georg Biro. Lazlo was a proof-reader and he got sick and tired of dipping his pen in ink every time he wanted to correct something. And of course, he was always nervous about spilling the ink on the precious manuscript.

Now I'll never know the end of the story!

He and brother Georg, were still working on their design for what they called a "writing stick" when World War II broke out, so they moved to Argentina and went on experimenting. By 1946, their new pens were selling in the USA and people were calling them biros. Lazlo and Georg had made it into the history books — and our dictionaries!

Just as well they weren't the Kölcsey brothers.

Or the Széchenyis!

Next in line were felt-tip pens and markers, so now we have an amazing choice of writing and drawing instruments. We've come a long way from fingers and sticks!

Wish they'd invent a pen that could spell!

87

Dear Mum and
Dad,
Goodbye.
I'm running away.
I love you.
I'll send you
a postcard.
Roger.

Leaving Home

I shifted around on my case so that I wasn't sitting on the handle any more. Ahhh ... that felt better. Some bus stops have seats, but not this one. All it had was a rusted-up old sign that didn't say anything any more, bolted to the end of a pole. The whole thing wobbled from side to side if you shook it.

I didn't bother doing that this time though; this was serious. I was taking one of those big steps in life. I was running away from home; starting a new life for myself.

I took another look around to make sure there was no one I knew. Yep, it was still safe. I had a disguise in my suitcase anyway, just in case somebody I knew started walking my way.

So far, so good.

This was the last Wednesday night I had before school started again. And it had to be on a Wednesday night, because that's the night my mum and dad go to the pictures and leave me at home with my two older sisters.

I had to move quick. By the time they'd walked from the house to the car, my case was packed. Then, while they were backing out the drive, I cut myself some sandwiches. I emptied out my money box, patted my dog goodbye for five minutes, and left a note on my bed.

Getting past my sisters was one of the easy parts. They're always acting like they've never seen me before.

So here I was at the bus stop. I'd left home almost ten minutes, and no bus. The more I sat there, the more I realised something. My plan wasn't perfect—I'd forgotten to find out when the bus came. And it wasn't as if I hadn't had long enough to find out when it came.

It all started—let me see, yes, it all started about a year ago.

The doctor had given me a week off school to spend with my virus. I was so sick I couldn't read, didn't feel like talking, and everything worth seeing on television I'd seen already. For two days I just sat in my bed and watched the picture rail go round and round.

Then my uncle Arthur came around with a box of magazines—travel magazines with pictures on every page. Boy were they interesting. I had to pretend I was sick for an extra week so I could finish 'em all.

When I went back to school again I tried to act normal and do all the old stuff I used to do, but something had happened inside me. I couldn't stop thinking about *places*.

So I started off just talking about leaving home then asking, then pleading, then back to just talking about it again. Thirty-five times a day (I kept count), seven days a week.

I stayed awake half my nights, just so I could pretend I was mumbling about it in my sleep. I covered my walls with pictures out of old *National Geographics*, went on a two-day hunger strike, and bought foreign maps for everyone on their birthdays.

"So you'll know where I am," I'd say.

But nobody understood me. I guess they just weren't my types. You know what I mean, not adventurers like me.

I hadn't seen anything. We went away every year to Dromana, but it never changed. The same shop, the same ice-creams in the shop. The caravan park was the same, the people in the caravans were the same.

And as if that wasn't bad, Peter Dusting was there as well. It wasn't enough that the nastiest, scariest, meanest and toughest kid in the school was in the same class as me, or lived in the next street to mine—but there he was, every year, just two caravans down from ours.

He had me so nervous I had to wait till he went down to the beach or some place before I could go anywhere. The worst part was never knowing what he'd do next.

A bucket of cold ice-water tipped over my head, my ice-cream pushed into my face, a herd of live soldier crabs set free in the annexe part where I slept, my clothes mixed up with someone else's every time I had a shower.

But at school he was worse. He had more time to think of things there. And he had regular nasty things that he'd do every day, like Chinese burns, or punching holes in my rain caps whenever it looked like rain, or the dumb notes he'd write about teachers with *my* name signed on the bottom. It was like being locked in the same room as a gorilla that hates you.

He'd just have to be standing near me when I was playing marbles and I'd miss, or look at me in class and bare his teeth, and my hands would go all sweaty.

He runs home every afternoon after school just so he can stand at his corner and make sure I don't take the short-cut down his stupid street. He has rules about his street. No Dagos, Turks, Japs or Poms allowed. When I told him I was born in Greece he just added "no Greeks either" to his list.

I crouched right over again and had another look at the clock in the milkbar across the road. I'd left home almost twenty minutes now, and still no bus.

I started thinking about the gang, I'd miss 'em and all that, but how else was I going to see the world, instead of just seeing Peter Dusting everywhere I went? And besides that, I'd never get to be famous hanging around Yarraville.

But once I did something daring, you know, like run away from home, or swim seventy kilometres with only one arm, then people would have to start talking. Roger Thesaurus would be a household name.

I looked up again, and there was a bus. It was one of the old types — slow as a snail and big as a mountain. It slowed down, grunted and hissed a couple of times, and stopped. I shoved my suitcase up the steps, then climbed up after it.

91

Nervous Neil was driving. He always looked a little bit too small to be driving a bus. Skinny body, skinny legs, skinny arms; he was skinny all over. His lips were so thin you could only see them when he opened his mouth to say something, and he had one of those noses that looked like a ski-jump.

He was full of nervous habits, like scratching his head, or trying to get some invisible piece of fluff from his bristly chin, or tapping his fingers on the steering wheel. And when he was really nervous he'd whistle, but it was always too fast for me to recognise the tune.

He was tapping his fingers.

"Railway station please Neil."

I put the right amount on the tray.

He gave the handle on his ticket machine two half turns, slammed the door shut and was off again. I picked up my suitcase and got to the back seat as soon as I could. Everybody sat up the back in Neil's bus.

It was a slow trip. I watched the traffic trying to pass us for a while, then looked at the other passengers to see if anyone was doing anything worth watching, then back to the traffic again. I pulled my money out of my pocket and counted it for the seventeenth time—$6.08 left after paying the bus fare. I put it back, then checked my shoelaces. Nothing to do there. The locks on the suitcase were still done up as well.

It felt like the slowest bus ride I'd ever had.

By the time we rattled up to the station I'd nearly had time to grow a beard.

We stopped and everyone made a polite leap for the door, the way adults do. I waited till there was just me and Neil left, then followed my bag down the aisle to where he was.

We'd never talked much, but I'd been getting off and on his bus since before I could walk.

"I don't suppose I'll be seeing you for a while, Neil," I said.

"Is that a fact?"

"You probably won't even recognise me next time you see me. I'm going away for a few years."

"Is that a fact?" he grumbled.

There wasn't much else to say. Neil wasn't much of a talker. So we just shook hands and said goodbye and all that. I promised him a postcard. I thought I'd probably send him one of those foreign traffic scenes. He'd enjoy that.

I only had to walk across the road, up the station ramp and I was there, at the ticket window.

There was a ticket seller I hadn't seen before. His face was all blotchy from freckles joining up here and there, and the spots without freckles were a pinky white colour. He looked a lot like an atlas of the world.

"A single to Sydney thanks," I said. I thought Sydney would be a good place to start.

"Sydney, eh?" He looked surprised. "Do your mum and dad know about this?"

"Sure."

All old people are the same. They won't believe you've got teeth unless you eat a three-course meal.

"Sydney, eh," he muttered again, and pulled out a little worn-out book from somewhere beside him. He flicked it till he came to a page near the back.

"The Sydney train doesn't arrive till tomorrow afternoon." He was smiling, like someone had just told him a joke or something.

"Tomorrow? . . . Are you sure?"

"No doubt about it."

I'd left home on the wrong day. How could I have been so stupid?

I looked up at the face behind the window. He was still smiling. I had an afternoon and a morning to spend just walking around. How could he be so happy? My sandwiches were going to get all squashed and soggy, my apples all bruised, before I even left Yarraville.

I turned and went back down the ramp and onto Neil's bus without really knowing that was what I was doing.

He was still sitting there, hunched up over the steering wheel, smoking his two-hundred-and-sixty-third cigarette for the day, waiting to make the return trip. He sat up, when he saw me.

"Now don't tell me, let me guess ... Is that old Roger Thesaurus? I almost didn't recognise you at first. I has been a long time, almost ... Almost eight minutes."

I knew he was going to say something like that. I ignored him and just said the first thing that came into my head.

"Single to Francis Street thanks."

I watched Neil crank the handle of his little machine, grabbed my tickets and forgot to pay. Then when I went back to pay I forgot my tickets. I was in a kind of dream. I couldn't get my head to work, it was blank up there—all my planning gone down the drain just like that.

I watched out the window till I could see Francis Street come up ahead. Slowly it was all coming to me. I knew why I'd said Francis Street—that's where Max lived. I'd got on the bus and paid the fare to Max's place out of habit.

That settled it. I'd spend the night there and catch the Sydney train tomorrow. He wouldn't mind.

I got out at the stop closest to Max's. With a bit of luck I could call out to him from the lane behind his place without anyone else knowing. I stopped beside the double gates where his dad used to take the car through, before there was too much junk in the yard for it to fit any more.

I found a paling missing and looked in. I could barely see the back of the house for all the junk—cardboard boxes, wooden boxes, old tins of mysterious black stuff, tyres without any tread left, rolls of worn-out lino, a pile of half-bricks, tables with wobbly legs, busted chairs. Max had it pretty good living amongst all that stuff.

I made sure that there was no one about before I called out.

"Hey Max," I half shouted, half whispered.   No answer.

"Hey Max." Louder that time.   Still nothing.

"Hey Max ... You there?" That was a yell.

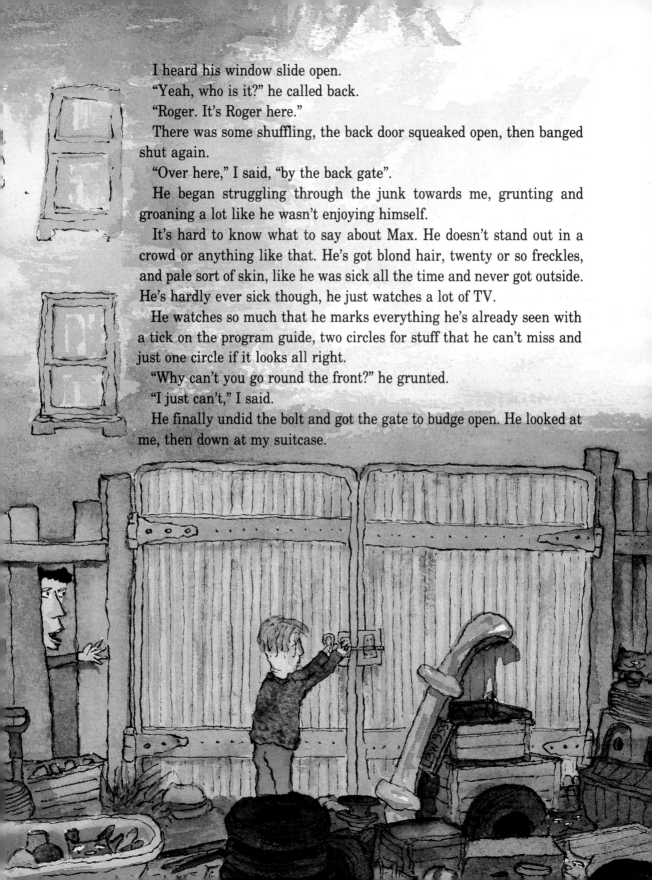

I heard his window slide open.

"Yeah, who is it?" he called back.

"Roger. It's Roger here."

There was some shuffling, the back door squeaked open, then banged shut again.

"Over here," I said, "by the back gate".

He began struggling through the junk towards me, grunting and groaning a lot like he wasn't enjoying himself.

It's hard to know what to say about Max. He doesn't stand out in a crowd or anything like that. He's got blond hair, twenty or so freckles, and pale sort of skin, like he was sick all the time and never got outside. He's hardly ever sick though, he just watches a lot of TV.

He watches so much that he marks everything he's already seen with a tick on the program guide, two circles for stuff that he can't miss and just one circle if it looks all right.

"Why can't you go round the front?" he grunted.

"I just can't," I said.

He finally undid the bolt and got the gate to budge open. He looked at me, then down at my suitcase.

"You come to move in or something?"

"Well it's a long story Max, I …"

He kept on looking back at his house like he had something important to do.

"Oh … well, can you make it short?" he said, glancing back at the house again. "There's a movie almost started; it's got Charlton Heston in it."

I told him the whole story about leaving home and stuff on the way up to the house. He stopped at the back door steps and said, "You haven't got too far yet".

"That's not my fault," I said. "I just need somewhere to sleep tonight and tomorrow morning I'll be gone."

He drew his eyebrows in so much that I thought he was going to make 'em touch each other for a moment. He let 'em go just at the last minute.

"Well … I guess you can stay in my room," he said at last.

"Thanks Max, I won't be no problem. You won't even know I'm here."

"But you'll have to lay low if any of my sisters come in for something."

(Max had six sisters.)

We shook on it, eased the back door open and stepped in. Max's was the first room on the left. It used to be the laundry before it was turned into the smallest bedroom in Melbourne. It was just like a big cardboard box lined with plaster—three and a half metres short and two metres narrow.

A wardrobe up one end which, compared to the room, was big enough to throw a party in, a bed on stilts so as he could sit underneath, an armchair that seemed to have some sort of disease, making it lose all of its stuffing and sending it bald, two stools, a lamp, a chest of drawers, a ladder, and a fifty-three-centimetre television. And that's just the stuff I can remember.

If you were careful enough you could move around without knocking something over. We shuffled ourselves around like a couple of semi-trailers doing a waltz on a miniature golf course.

96

Once we got settled in, we took it in turns to sit in the sick armchair. A half an hour each.

The movie finished and Charlton Heston won the battle, "Gilligan's Island" came and went, then "Hogan's Heroes", "The Odd Couple", "Bonanza" ...

It had gotten dark outside, and there we were, still watching TV. My eyes had begun to go all blurred and fuzzy and I was getting a headache. I tried making conversation once or twice but Max only liked talking in the advertisement breaks. So we just went on sitting there like a couple of stunned mullets.

We even sat through an antique re-run of the "Dean Martin Show", without moaning or booing once. I'd caught the "stuck where you are, can't move, don't talk, big dummy in the chair" disease.

When the "Dean Martin Show" finished we swapped positions. This time I got the armchair and Max got the cushion. He grabbed the guide and checked it over again.

"Guess what's on now, Rog'? — 'The Elevator' ... You'll love it."
"Oh?"
"Yeah, listen to what it's about. Two guys have just robbed a jeweller's on the seventeenth floor and they get stuck in it, and the jeweller's secretary chases them and she gets stuck as well ..."

He was talking right in the middle of an ad for kitchen furniture.

"... and just to make things complicated," he went on, "she used to be married to one of the robbers as well".

"The programme guide tells you all that?" I asked.

"No, I've seen it before, about six months ago. 'Cept I had a bad cold and my nose was runnin' so bad ..."

Suddenly Max was up on his feet and over at his door. He pressed his ear against it.

"What is it?" I said.

"Somebody's coming," he said. "Quick, hide in the wardrobe. I'll get rid of whoever it is."

It was dark in there. I felt my way into one of the doors and slid it shut after me. I left myself a gap about as wide as a pencil so I could breathe through, then crouched down.

Max had just jumped back into his chair when the door opened and somebody walked in. It was one of his sisters. It looked like Lorraine, the second oldest. She mumbled something about their dad watching the other TV and how boring it was. Max mumbled something, she mumbled something back, and then sat down.

Then ... squeak ... it was Max's door again. This time it was Dolores, another sister. Before she had time to sit down there was somebody else thumping about out there. It was another sister. I couldn't see who. Maybe it was more than one.

Oh no! Suddenly they were all in there. All six of them — sitting down there, squatting on cushions here, climbing up onto the bed, swinging their legs around.

"What is Max doing out there?" I thought. *"What happened to his 'I'll get rid of whoever it is' promise?"*

I could see bits and pieces of all of them from where I was. They were practically sitting on top of each other. They must have felt terrible, because I felt about as comfortable as a dirty old hanky bunched up in someone's pocket, but at least I could stretch my legs out.

The minutes turned into quarter of an hour each, then halves of hours, then hours. Time was dragging on, and, besides that, I was sure I could smell something. I hadn't noticed it before, but the longer I spent crouched up in there the stronger it got.

I couldn't decide if it was more like rotten eggs, or a busted sewage pipe underneath me somewhere. Or then again, maybe something had died in Max's wardrobe and he'd forgotten to take it out. But whatever it was, it was getting stronger. I could feel the hair up my nose wilting.

I couldn't see a thing, so there was no point in looking. I started feeling around with my hands and then holding things up to my nose.

There were a lot of soft things, some bottle tops, a tennis ball, pencils with broken points, a pile of books in one corner, a cup with no handle, a handle with no cup ... Then I found it.

It was hairy, and long, and had a sort of mouth at one end. I held it up to my nose and almost fainted. Phew, it was strong.

Hang on! I found another one. Two of them. A pair ... Socks! A pair of Max's horrible socks. They were disgusting and putrid, and so dirty they'd gone stiff at the toe end.

I felt around some more. They were everywhere. HELP! I was sitting smack bang in the middle of Max's rest home for old and used socks.

He must have had thirty pairs there and they were all as bad as each other. There was no escaping them. Everywhere I turned now I found another sock.

I had to get my mind off them, had to think about something else. I tried to think about happy things like Christmas Day, and my next birthday, but it was no good. I couldn't concentrate with all that smell going on. And besides, my lips were getting cramps from trying to squeeze them into the little gap for some fresh air.

Finally the movie finished, but nobody moved out there. Then came a bunch of ads, and they just sat right through them, eyes glued to the set.

I heard another movie start.

"It looks like a Western," I heard Dolores say.

"You don't mind, Max, if we stay in here and watch do you?"

"Well as a matter of fact ..." Max started to say.

"Oh good. Thanks Max. We won't be any bother," somebody else said. "But you just tell us if you want to go to bed."

"Well as a matter of fact I am a bit sleepy ..."

"You're really something special Max."

"Yeah, thanks Max."

"We're lucky to have a brother like Max."

They were really laying it on thick, nodding their heads up and down and all agreeing amongst themselves about how special Max was. I felt like being sick.

"Max, how could you do this to me? Some of these Westerns go on forever."

"Gone With The Wind" took three hours to finish once it had started.

I was feeling worse. My face was all hot and sweating. My stomach felt like a dance floor, my legs had the jitters, my eyes were watering, and there was a lump in my throat. I was losing control. I was going to be sick for sure. I couldn't breathe. My stomach was about to ...

I couldn't stand it any more.

I stuck my fingers into the gap between the door and the wall and slid it open with a bang.

Saved! From death by unbelievable smells.

I fell out sideways, rolled around a bit, managed to find the bed post and sat up leaning against it. I closed my eyes and just breathed for a while. Lungful after lungful of pure, clean, wonderful air.

I opened my eyes. Nobody was watching the TV any more.

"My, the air is sure good out here," I said.

No one said anything. They all just stared at me like surprised shop dummies, mouths open, eyes as big as saucepans—I'd seen more life in the rock specimens at the museum.

Max looked the worst of all. His mouth had dropped open so much that I thought it might have fallen off altogether.

I stood up, grabbed my suitcase from behind the TV and opened the door to go.

"Well thanks for the loan of your wardrobe Max. But I couldn't find that compass you reckoned was in there." It was the best thing I could think of to say.

Max looked at me as if there was something he wanted to say, but his mouth didn't want to do anything about it.

I kept on walking till I was out in the lane at the back of Max's. Nothing had gone right. I'd gone for the train on the wrong day, I had nowhere to sleep, and now Max would probably get into trouble.

I was a failure. A stupid, no-good, dumb, dense idiot. What was the sense in living? I couldn't do anything right. A simple thing like leaving home and I'd muffed it. I was in Spotswood. That's further away from Sydney than where I set off from. What sort of an idiot would end up six kilometres farther away?

Written by Max Dann
Illustrated by Terry Denton

When I'm Thirteen

1 When I'm thir-teen__ I'm gon-na start a band__ With a
drum kit, bass and a sax-o-phone__ and me as the gui-tar__man.__ We'll
play at Sul-li-van's Dis - co ev-'ry Sat-ur-day night__ and
maybe__ rock on__ TV when the time is - right.

v.3 to ending | v. 1, 2.

When I'm thir-teen__ I'm gon-na start a band.__

Doop der doop, next Oct-o-ber, Doop der doop I'll be old-er. -
Doop der doop, come Oct-o-ber, I'll be thir - teen.

Doop der doop, start that rock band, Doop der doop, sing on TV

From ✵ to ending

Doop der doop, I won-der what my dad will say, "O-kay".__

⊕ ENDING

I've got a rock 'n roll band,__ I've got a rock 'n roll band,__

__ I've got a rock 'n roll band,__ Doop der doop!

102

Peter Combe

2 When I'm thirteen, I'm gonna set the beat,
   With soul at the disco and bop-a-long in the street.
   So kick up your heels start dancing,
   Say goodbye to the day,
   Get with the rock and rollin',
   Grooving the night away.
   When I'm thirteen, I'm gonna set the beat.
   Doop der doop, next October,
   Doop der doop, I'll be older,
   Doop der doop, come October, I'll be thirteen.
   Doop der doop, start that rock band,
   Doop der doop, sing on TV,
   Doop der doop, I wonder what my dad will say: "Okay"

3 Now I'm thirteen and I've got a rock 'n' roll band,
   And every Friday we get together and jam.
   There's Donald on the drumkit,
   Billy playing the bass,
   There's Sally on the saxophone,
   And me I'm the guitar man.
   Now I'm thirteen, and I've got a rock 'n' roll band,
                    I've got a rock 'n' roll band,
                    I've got a rock 'n' roll band —
                    Doop der doop!

HOW TO STAY UNHEALTHY!

Spending time in a stuffy wardrobe full of smelly socks is one way ... but there are others!

1 Exercise twice a year to achieve muscle strain and back pain! Wonderful!

2 Don't bother with activities which will improve strength, stamina and suppleness. Stick to playing marbles.

3 Don't stand when you can sit. Don't sit when you can lie. Be a slob.

4 Install every possible kind of labour-saving device so you'll never have to get up to change TV channels, open garage doors, chop up a cabbage ... ever, ever, ever again.

5 Drive everywhere. Never walk.

6 Eat lots and lots and lots of refined fast food. Snack regularly at the local takeaway shop. Throw out all brown bread and fresh vegies. Clog up your body and develop lots of pimples.

7 Sleep? That's strictly for the birds. Stay up late so your body has no chance to rest. Wear it out.

What a dumb T-shirt you've got.

SMILE

But we only ate :
6 Hamburgers
4 Packets of Chips
2 Icecreams
5 Fizzy drinks
10 Hotdogs
everyday for a
whole year !

8 Never laugh and enjoy yourself — leave that to the kookaburras. Instead, practise moaning and griping. Become a pessimist. Depress all your friends as well as yourself. Be mean.

If you carefully follow all eight steps, we guarantee you will become an excellently miserable and unhealthy person. It's YOUR choice. You can be different !

105

WORST FRIEND

OR

BEST ENEMY?

Adapted from the Aesop fable *The Travellers and the Bear.*
By **Pat Edwards** · Illustrated by **Peter Foster.**

One day two friends were travelling a road together.

Nothing like a walk in the countryside with a good friend.

107

Then he took to his heels and ran for the nearest tree.

I should just have time to climb this tree.

After I'm safe in the tree I'll throw some leaves at the bear!

Help! Don't leave me!

Unable to escape the second man threw himself flat and pretended to be dead, for he'd heard a bear will never touch a dead body.

Alas, I'm probably done for!

SNIFF!

SNIFF!

108

I hope one person fills him up!

SNIFF!

Bravely, he held his breath and kept st
while the bear sniffed his nose and ea

…nd to his great joy and amazement the bear slowly walked on.

It's alright, friend, we're *safe!*

Oh, HONEY, be my honey bee! ♪

I can't believe it!

You know, old chap, it almost looked as if that bear was whispering something in your ear.

He ***was!*** He was warning me not to go around with people who abandon their friends as soon as there's a spot of trouble.

Goodbye!!!

?!

MORAL

Trouble and misfortune will soon tell you who your true friends are.

109

Picking Teams

When we pick teams in the playground,
Whatever the game might be,
There's always somebody left till last
And usually it's me.

I stand there looking hopeful
And tapping myself on the chest,
But the captains pick the others first,
Starting, of course, with the best.

Maybe if teams were sometimes picked
Starting with the worst,
Once in his life a boy like me
Could end up being first!

Words to pick

Glossary

antacid tablet (*p.12*)
tablet for stomach pain

artificial (*p.66*)
not natural, made by people

astigmatism (*p.52*)
focussing problem of the eyes

co-ed school (*p.8*)
a mixed secondary school for both boys and girls

drugstore (*p.63*)
an American name for a chemist's shop which often sells sweets and magazines

ebbed (*p.41*)
faded away

ecstatically (*p.17*)
with delight and happiness

epoxy resin (*p.15*)
very strong glue

etymology (*p.49*)
the study of words

flinch (*p.8*)
shrink back from something nasty

gastro-enteritis (*p.12*)
painful stomach upset

Gestetner (*p.12*)
spiritmaster duplicating machine — old fashioned form of photocopying

hectoring (*p.12*)
ordering in a bossy way

horde (*p.8*)
a very large group

Hubbard Squash (*p.50*)
orange-coloured vegetable

humiliation (*p.18*)
feeling awful about yourself

inept (*p.65*)
unable to do anything

insolent (*p.15*)
rude, insulting

Letraset *(p.15)*
sheets of letters that can be rubbed onto paper — like transfers

macrame *(p.6)*
weaving and knotting string into patterns

milkbar *(p.91)*
a cafe serving ice-cream, drinks and snacks

mullets *(p.97)*
kind of fish

nauseating *(p.55)*
causing a feeling of sickness

obscene *(p.19)*
disgusting

paling *(p.94)*
one of the wooden planks making up a fence

pantomimed *(p.70)*
pretended

pessimist *(p.105)*
a person who looks at the worst side of every situation

serenity *(p.18)*
a feeling of peace

skittering *(p.14)*
darting, moving lightly and rapidly

snitchy *(p.7)*
annoyed or cross

solitary *(p.18)*
lonely

stanching *(p.40)*
trying to stop

tarradiddle *(p.41)*
a small lie

tedious *(p.19)*
annoying in a boring way

viciously *(p.12)*
bad-tempered